Better Homes and Gardens.

from Garden *to* Plate

Meredith® Consumer Marketing

Better Homes and Gardens® *From Gareden to Plate*
Editor: Karen Weir-Jimerson
Designer: Sundie Ruppert
Art Directors: Ken Carlson, Waterbury Publications, Inc.; Tim Alexander
Research Assistants: Loral Jagman, Chance Dorland
Copy Editor: Peg Smith
Proofreaders: Terri Frederickson, Gretchen Kauffman
Indexer: Elizabeth T. Parson

Better Homes and Gardens® *Magazine*
Editor in Chief: Gayle Goodson Butler
Editor in Chief, Gardening: Doug Jimerson
Executive Editor: Kitty Morgan
Managing Editor: Lamont D. Olson
Art Director: Michael D. Belknap

Meredith National Media Group
President: Tom Harty
Executive Vice President: Doug Olson
Vice President, Manufacturing: Bruce Heston
Vice President, Consumer Marketing: David Ball
Director, Consumer Product Marketing: Kathi Prien
Director, Production: Douglas M. Johnston
Business Manager: Ron Clingman

Meredith Corporation
Chairman, President, and Chief Executive Officer: Stephen M. Lacy
In Memoriam: E.T. Meredith III (1933-2003)

Contributing Photographers:
Adam Albright, King Au, Quentin Bacon, Marty Baldwin, André Baranowski, Edmund Barr, Matthew Benson, Laurie Black, Jessica Boone, Bruce Buck, Rob Cardillo, Kim Cornelison, Stephen Cridland, Kip Dawkins, Mike Dieter, Jason Donnelly, Colleen Duffley, John Reed Forsman, Michael Garland, Susan Gilmore, Tria Giovan, Tony Glaser, Ed Gohlich, David Goldberg, Leo Gong, Justin Hancock, Chipper R. Hatter, William N. Hopkins, Bill Hopkins, Robert Jacobs, Michael Jensen, Richard Jung, Dency Kane, Lynn Karlin, Jeff Kauck, Layne Kennedy, Peter Krumhardt, Jennifer Levy, Jason Lindsey, Scott Little, Andy Lyons, Julie Maris Semarco, Bryan E. McCay, Alison Miksch, Blaine Moats, John Noitner, Kritsada Panichgul, Jerry Pavia, Frank Peairs@Colorado State University, Bugwood.org, Celia Pearson, Eric Roth, Tina Rupp, Greg Scheidemann, Dean Schoeppner, Bob Stefko, Ann Stratton, Steve Struce, C. Trouvé@Service de la Protection des Végétaux, Bugwood.org, Jay Wilde

Contributing Garden Illustrators:
Mavis Torke, Tom Rosborough

Contributing Cover Photographers:
Bill Stites, Marty Baldwin, Andy Lyons, Scott Little, Peter Krumhardt

Copyright® *2010 by Meredith Corporation. Des Moines, Iowa*
First Edition. All rights reserved.
Printed in the United States of America
ISBN: 978-0-696-30017-2

All of us at Meredith Consumer Marketing are dedicated to providing you with information and ideas to enhance your home and garden.
We welcome your comments and suggestions. Write to us at:
Meredith Consumer Marketing
1716 Locust Street
Des Moines, IA 50309-3023

Note to the readers: Due to differing conditions, tools, and individual skills, Meredith Corporation assumes no responsibility for any damages, injuries suffered, or losses incurred as a result of following the information published in this book. Before beginning any project, review the instructions carefully, and if any doubts or questions remain, consult local experts or authorities. Because codes and regulations vary greatly, you should always check with authorities to ensure that your project complies with all applicable local codes and regulations. Always read and observe all of the safety precautions provided by manufacturers of any tools, equipment, or supplies, and follow all accepted safety procedures.

Pictured on the front cover:
Tomato and Mint Salad, recipe page 84

Chapter 1

Chapter 2

Chapter 3

Contents

Grow Your Own Food

Raising food has never been easier—or more fun. And growing food right out your back door means harvesting and meal preparation is more convenient than ever.

Welcome to great taste! And the freshest food you'll ever eat. Whether you grow crops from seeds or plant seedlings in your garden, once you raise a few of your own crops (and see how easy and tasty they are), you'll expand your garden year after year. Here are some of the reasons you'll enjoy growing, harvesting, and preparing your own fresh foods.

Count the choices

With the diverse selection of fruit and vegetable varieties, you can grow foods you see in grocery stores—or delve into a wide and flavorful world of heirloom and specialty varieties. With hundreds of tomatoes to choose from, don't settle for tasteless, juiceless, nondescript ones. New, improved, and disease-resistant varieties make growing vegetables easier than ever. Enjoy the flavors of the past by growing heirloom varieties.

Improve old recipes with fresh ingredients or make less-complicated recipes with ingredients that have fresh and dynamic flavors of their own.

Behold the beauty

Food gardens can be beautiful. They can, but don't have to be, utilitarian plots of straight rows. Incorporate fruit and vegetables into the landscapes, along with flowers, trees, and shrubs. Grow leafy chard next to blooming delphiniums. Edge annual flowerbeds with strawberries. Anchor a garden bed with a fountain of onion foliage. Fruit trees, laden with ripening apples or pears, can be front-yard trees. Discovering good things to eat as you wander through your front- or backyard makes gardening a hobby of surprises, flavors, and scents.

Enchant and educate kids

Food gardening is enticing to children, who may be more eager to eat sweet fresh peas straight from the garden yet turn up their noses at the frozen or canned versions. Let them pluck juicy berries from beneath umbrellalike leaves or pull baby carrots out of the ground like buried treasure.

Studies show that kids who plant vegetables and fruits have a positive attitude toward these foods. Consuming more fruits and vegetables—especially homegrown varieties—is a healthful way to eat. Starting out kids with good eating habits is key to a healthy life. Because childhood obesity has nearly tripled in the past 20 years, offering healthful foods and snacks is more important than ever. Some studies point to the possibility that

kids do better academically when gardening is part of their life or school curriculum.

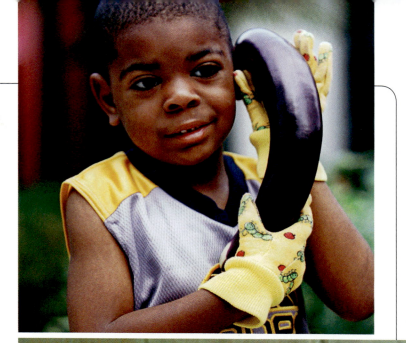

Reap nutritional superiority
Besides eating more fruits and vegetables (and why not, when they are just steps from the back door?), the produce from your own garden may have more nutrients than foods from the store because they are fresher—at the peak of goodness. Grocery store produce may have traveled thousands of miles to reach market shelves, with nutrient goodness diminished en route or because of handling and packaging.

Savor simple and safe goodness
Gardeners who grow organic food know what type of soil and amendments the food has been grown in. If you choose to raise food organically, you can be confident that no pesticides or herbicides were sprayed on your food. The delicious results are healthful, safe foods.

Stretch, breathe, and be aware
Gardening, especially food gardening, is one way to get moderate exercise while being outdoors in the sunshine and fresh air, with the bonus of sweet nibbles from the garden. The simple act of planting seeds or weeding beds offers stretching and bending that are good for backs, legs, and arms. A daily walk around the garden to check for pests and monitor what to harvest is also exercise. From a spiritual perspective, what can be more enjoyable than partaking in the pleasures of your garden? Sowing seeds, tending veggies, and bringing in a bountiful harvest bring you closer to the cycles and seasons of life.

Garden well—regardless of space
You don't need a lot of space to raise fruits and vegetables. Container gardening means that anyone—with or without a yard—can grow strawberries, lettuces, herbs, and even small trees in containers. Many gardeners who have adequate space add containers or window boxes to the mix because they can be conveniently located near the kitchen door: What can be fresher tasting than clipped rosemary or basil added to hot pasta and olive oil?

Save money and feel more in control

Many people raise food crops simply to save money on weekly grocery bills. Why not? A packet of seeds can cost as little as $1. If you check recent prices on packaged herbs or mixed greens, you'll see how much you can save when you plant and grow these high-price items. For families who like to eat organic, raising organic food in the backyard or in containers on a patio or terrace saves even more on this expensive trend. Organic food often tastes better, but it costs more. Here's the clincher—raising food organically at home is the most inexpensive way to garden because expensive pesticides and herbicides aren't applied.

Growing a garden also helps you feel in control. At the end of the day, when you return to your little plot of green veggies and pluck a green salad, a sun-ripened tomato, and a curvy cucumber, all seems right in the world.

Prepare bistro-quality meals

Trendy bistro-style eateries are renowned for serving the highest quality fresh, and often locally grown and organic, foods. You can too! Fresh herbs, sun-warmed peppers and tomatoes, and crisp greens are premium ingredients served elegantly simple in dishes that showcase bright color, fresh flavor, and distinct texture. The freshest produce requires minimal preparation. Let it stand out by presenting it as uncomplicated as possible. The fresh goodness will shine through.

Chapter 2

Make a Garden

Fruit, vegetable, and herb gardens can be as beautiful as they are edible. With a good plan, your food garden can be as colorful, textural, and inspirational as a flower garden.

Modern kitchen gardens borrow design techniques from medieval gardens: square or rectangular beds and a path that bisects the garden.

From the design of the garden to the beauty of the plants to the bountiful harvest, a fruit, herb, and vegetable garden is so satisfying. Called kitchen gardens, for the obvious reason that they provide foods for the kitchen, these plots of produce may change the way you cook and eat.

The first kitchen gardens

Following the classic kitchen garden design, the vegetable garden (*opposite*) in Colonial Williamsburg features symmetrical beds packed with a variety of produce.

Kitchen gardens, still popular today, date back several thousand years, hailing from all cultures. Accounts from history show that kitchen gardens were integral in aspects of life across the globe.

From early Chinese records, we learn that medicinal herb gardens were cultivated as early as the third millennium B.C. By 2700 B.C., Egyptians had recorded growing more than 500 herbs. A small Egyptian painting in the British Museum, dated circa 1400 B.C., shows the garden of Nebamun, rectangular with a suggestion of a stone border. In the pond, are waterfowl, flowers, and fish. Date palms form a symmetrical pattern around the pond.

In the ancient Middle East, pleasure gardens were beautiful yet practical. Walls protected the house from marauders and warmed the gardens. Buffered by the walls, exotic plants grew that would not otherwise grow in that climate. A pond in the center of the garden was a source of water for the garden and home to fish raised as food for the table.

Several documents dating back to the reign of Charlemagne (about 800 A.D.) describe gardens of the era. From the perspective of kitchen gardens, the most significant is the plan for a Swiss monastery. Four rectangular gardens, each with its own purpose, were laid out within a square cloister. The physic garden (medicinal herb garden), which was located close to the infirmary, had 16 separate planting beds laid out in two rows of nine. Another garden featured symmetrically planted fruit trees.

Medieval gardens

Built either square or rectangular, medieval gardens shared specific details. A wall or fence, often a high wattle fence, enclosed the garden. Crossing paths bisected each garden, dividing each into similar shape beds or gardens. This pleasing design formed the basis for formal gardens later developed in Europe.

How do kitchen gardens differ from vegetable gardens laid out in a series of rows? Kitchen gardens combine form and function, beauty and practicality.

English gardens

Early English kitchen gardens were based on a foursquare layout, with simple design providing ease of culture for herbs, vegetables, grains, and fruit to grow together. It also created a rich yet unpretentious display of color and form. Flowers crept into the garden to add a touch of beauty.

Symmetry often gave way to practicality—paths were offset when required. Allowances were made for doors, windows, or entrances. A wall of some sort enclosed the garden, forerunner of the modern outdoor "room." As in the gardens that preceded them, the walls were functional, protecting the garden, creating a warmer microclimate in which to grow a wide range of edibles. Originally the gate was a practical part of the design, forming the entryway into the garden through the wall. Today gates are design elements, giving gardens a distinct style.

Your kitchen garden

Design your kitchen garden to suit your planting site, growing foods in the variety and amounts that you can handle. Combining beautiful vegetables with fragrant herbs, glistening fruits, and annual and perennial flowers creates a garden that pleases the eye as much as the palate.

Loam is the ideal soil. It holds nutrients, drains well, and is easy to plant in.

Getting Started

Plants need sun, water, and nutrients. An area that gets at least six hours of sun a day is the best site for a kitchen garden. Most vegetables benefit from more sun—except in the hot South, where selective shading in summer is beneficial.

Natural rainfall may be enough water for some plants, but most vegetables benefit from supplemental watering. There are many ways to provide plants with water—low-tech or high-tech. In a small garden a simple watering can or hose-end sprinkler is often the simplest way to water. A computerized, in-ground irrigation system represents the opposite end of the spectrum.

Making sense of soil

Soil is the seemingly magic substrate that anchors plants in place and supplies many of their nutritional needs. Yet many novice gardeners seem most intimidated by soil.

Sand, like the sand at the beach, has a very loose structure—water runs right through it. Clay, on the other hand, retains water. The same holds true for sandy and clay soil.

Type of soil is determined by relative amounts of sand, clay, and silt contained by the soil. The best soils have some sand, some silt, and a little clay. Referred to as loams, these soils hold nutrients, drain adequately, and are easy to work with. They are loose enough for roots to easily penetrate.

Your soil

Different areas of the country have distinct soil types. Two simple, at-home tests will determine the physical properties of garden soil.

The easiest and quickest is the squeeze test. Take a handful of slightly moist garden soil and gently squeeze it. Open your hand and look at the soil. Sandy soil won't hold any shape; it crumbles and falls easily through your fingers. Clay forms a tight ball, retaining the squeeze marks. Loam is between sand and clay; it seems to conform to your hand shape and is a ball, yet crumbly on the edges.

The second way to determine soil type is the jar method. Combine ½ cup of soil with 1½ cups of water in a glass jar. Cover the jar and shake vigorously, enough to loosen the soil and move it through the water. The soil components will settle in different ways. Sand settles quickly to the bottom of the jar—measure its height after one minute. Silt is the next to settle on the sand—measure its height after one hour. The final component, clay, settles on the silt—measure it after one day. When the layers of silt and sand are the same size as the layer of clay, the soil is good

and loamy. Some experts suggest that the best loam is about 20 percent clay and 40 percent each silt and sand. If the soil has more sand, it is sandy loam.

Improving and enhancing

If your garden doesn't have perfect soil, don't despair. You can improve the soil by adding organic matter. Leaf mold, compost, and well-rotted manure are the best amendments for improving soil structure. Add these soil amendments when preparing the garden for planting. They are also useful as top dressing to spread around plants in the garden, acting as both mulch and slow-release fertilizer. Organic mulches, such as pinestraw and cocoa and barley hulls, break down over time and benefit the soil.

Amend the soil by adding peat moss or compost before you plant.

Amend your soil to grow more robust and healthy crops.

No-dig gardening

Digging and rototilling can overwork the soil. By constantly working the soil, there is the danger of breaking down the structure into dustlike powder or hardening it like concrete. Many gardeners never rototill or turn the soil. Instead they prepare the beds in the fall for spring planting by spreading as much as 12 inches of organic matter on the beds. Any organic matter, such as compost, hay, oak leaves (shredded are best), sawdust, pine needles, shredded newspapers, manure, vegetable scraps, and peat moss works. Moisten the whole area, add a little agricultural lime, and wait for it to break down.

Soil is easily worked the following spring. Simply push aside the mulch and plant seeds or seedlings. Continuously replenish the mulch, and the soil will get better and better. This approach also saves time-consuming weeding.

Do not dig or work the soil when it is overly dry or wet. In spring use the squeeze test to determine when the soil is ready to be worked. If the soil forms a loose ball that falls apart when poked, it's ready to dig or plant.

Fertilizer

Amend garden soil with compost, well-rotted manure, or leaf mold (all organic), or choose from a variety of manufactured fertilizers. Each package of fertilizer has three numbers printed on it, whether it is organic, inorganic, or chemical fertilizer. The numbers, such as 20-20-20, represent the N-P-K ratio, or percentage of those specific macronutrients. A 100-pound bag labeled 5-10-5 contains the following: 5 pounds of nitrogen (N), 10 pounds of phosphorus (P), and 5 pounds of potassium (K). Individual crops may call for special formulas of fertilizer, which is easy to apply.

Water

Plants generally are more than 90 percent water and need a steady supply to perform their best. Vegetables need proper moisture levels from seedling stage through harvest.

The frequency of watering depends on several factors. Sandy soils or hot, sunny locations need more water than clay soils or shady spots. Weather also changes plants' needs for water. Plants in cloudy or cool conditions demand less water than those in hot and sunny areas. Some crops need more water than others. Leafy vegetables need more water than root vegetables.

Whenever you water, thoroughly soak the plants' root systems. For seedlings or young plants, soak to a depth of only a few inches. Deep-rooted plants need soaking to a much greater depth.

Although sprinklers and hoses can provide lots of summer fun, they are not the best choices for watering vegetables, herbs, and flowers in a kitchen garden. A better option is to install drip irrigation systems—some have timers and computerized controls and have special emitters to release water gradually to individual plants so the water slowly soaks the soil.

A weepy hose or leaky pipe hose slowly leaks water from all sides. Lay it around large plants or between rows and either keep the hose uncovered or bury it beneath a 2-inch layer of mulch.

Sprinklers, although portable and easily placed, lose water to evaporation. The water goes on the plant, not necessarily at soil level to soak in for the roots to absorb. Water early in the morning so the leaves will dry in the warmth of the sun. Late-day watering promotes fungus and disease, because leaves remain wet through the night.

Furrow watering, although not commonly done, is a good way to irrigate perennial plantings, such as asparagus. This type of watering works only on level ground in soil that is not sandy. Design the garden with furrows between the raised beds. To work well, the raised areas should be no more than 4 feet across, and the furrows 1 foot wide and 6 inches deep. Slowly flood the furrows, then dam off a section to allow the water to penetrate.

Mulch

Any material spread on the soil to prevent weeds from growing keep soil temperatures even and help retain soil moisture is considered mulch. Many plants benefit with a thick layer of mulch at their roots, which prevents soil-borne diseases from splashing on the leaves. Using as much as 6 inches of organic mulch at the base of tomato plants, for example, prevents many diseases. Organic mulch breaks down, becomes part of, and improves the soil.

Shredded newspapers, leaves, grass clippings (add it an inch at a time or it will become slimy and not break down), straw, well-rotted manure, and compost allow water to penetrate while controlling weeds. Depending on where you live, you may be able to get cocoa hulls, ground corncobs, peanut hulls, pecan hulls, pine needles, salt hay, sawdust, straw, or wood shavings. All freshly processed wood by-products, such as bark and sawdust, can also be used.

Black plastic sheeting, which helps warm the soil in spring and provides a head start on planting, is especially useful for heat-loving crops. Spread it out and cut holes to plant seedlings. Provide irrigation to plants with a drip system or a soaker hose placed beneath the plastic.

Tomatoes are warm-weather crops and must be planted after your area's last frost date. Knowing the hardiness zone and frost dates for your garden is important for a successful kitchen garden.

Plan your kitchen garden

If you have a small area for a kitchen garden, build raised beds and use vertical structures such as tepees or fencing to grow vining crops such as peas and beans.

Plan your garden to make the best use of your time and space. It is often best to start small, plan carefully, and maintain that space well for a season. Then decide how much more (or less) space you want to devote to the garden next season. Even with labor-saving approaches, each square foot of space added to the plan means more work in the garden.

Choose a sunny site

Almost all fruits and vegetables grow well in full sun. Site a kitchen garden where it receives a minimum of six hours of sunlight each day. Don't assume that the area is totally sunny: Look at it at different times of the day. If you plan the garden during winter, the garden may seem sunny. If there are deciduous trees nearby, the garden may be shaded when the trees leaf out. Also note shade from shrubs, buildings, fences, and other structures.

A location near the kitchen is ideal for a cook to easily pop into the garden to harvest fresh vegetables or snip herbs for a meal in progress. A nearby site will get used more, and a well-used garden will produce the greatest satisfaction.

Choose a site free of competing roots from trees and shrubs that would steal nutrients. Because vegetables need frequent watering, a source of water should be nearby. A spigot at the edge of the garden is ideal, although a site reachable with a length or two of hose will work.

Plant with hardiness in mind

Before designing your garden, recognize your physical limits as well as the limits of the climate where you live. A kitchen garden has a broader scope than the typical vegetable garden with fruit trees, shrubs, and perennials. These plants will remain in the garden for many years, unlike most vegetables, which are grown as annuals.

When buying permanent plants—anything other than annuals—know your hardiness zone before purchasing plants to survive winter. The USDA Hardiness Zone map on page 230 shows the 10 hardiness zones for North America. Find your zone, then choose trees, shrubs, and perennials that are hardy in that zone.

Within any property, there are microclimates. If your kitchen garden has a wall around it, it may be a zone warmer than the rest of the property. An exposed area, on the other hand, may be a zone cooler. Use the microclimates to your advantage to grow more and varied plants. When planning the garden, also pay attention to the last frost date in spring and the first frost date in autumn.

Spreading organic matter on the soil and raking it smooth makes the bed easy to plant in.

French Potager Garden

This French Normandy-inspired property includes a delightful side yard of vegetables and herbs that provide months of garden-fresh meals.

The French long ago learned to make productive use of every inch of garden space. Unlike many Americans, Europeans for centuries have had to cope with limited land.

This potager, or kitchen garden, is a charming example of how Europeans overcame the problem of gardening in a small space. Measuring only 6 feet deep by 16 feet long, the raised bed is defined in whitewashed brick to match the house.

The raised bed is filled with a blend of compost and good-quality topsoil. Trellises are painted the same lavender-blue as the shutters and planted with small climbing roses that remain under 10 feet tall.

The trumpet vine in the corner will sprawl up the side of the house 40 feet or more. In tighter quarters, clematis or another rose would be a better choice. (Note: Trumpet vine is not edible. The roses and marigolds, however, are edible. Use petals of either in salads or as a garnish for drinks and desserts.)

Set out transplants of lettuces or save money and sow seeds directly in the row, thinning seedlings to the correct spacing. Use the excess thinned seedlings, those not transplanted, as tender baby lettuce greens.

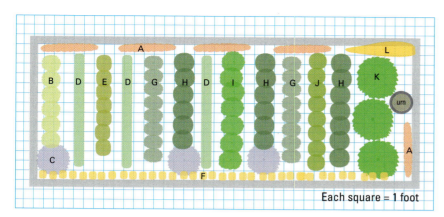

Each square = 1 foot

Tuck a highly productive vegetable and fruit garden in a space no larger than a small strip alongside the house.

PLANT LIST

A. **5 Climbing roses** such as 'Joseph's Coat': Zones 5–9

B. **6 Looseleaf lettuces** (*Lactuca sativa*) such as 'Salad Bowl': Annual

C. **3 Lavenders** (*Lavandula angustifolia*): Zones 5–10

D. **45 Onions** (*Allium cepa*): Annual

E. **7 Butterhead lettuces** (*Lactuca sativa* 'Bibb'): Annual

F. **35 French marigolds** (*Tagetes patula*): Annual

G. **16 Spinaches** (*Spinacea oleracea*) such as 'Melody': Annual

H. **19 Romaine lettuces** (*Lactuca sativa*) such as 'Parris Island Cos': Annual

I. **7 Looseleaf lettuces** (*Lactuca sativa*) such as 'Black Seeded Simpson': Annual

J. **8 Spinaches** (*Spinacia oleracea*) such as 'Tyee': Annual

K. **3 Korean boxwoods** (*Buxus sinica* 'Wintergreen'): Zones 5–9

L. **1 Yellow trumpet vine** (*Campsis radicans* 'Flava'): Zones 5–9

Raised Bed Garden

This garden is a food machine, producing abundant harvests for many meals. It also includes annual and perennial flowers that contribute color and fragrance in the garden or for flower arrangements.

Gardeners often relegate vegetables to one section of the garden and flowers to another. Yet in garden design, there are no rules for separating the two. Some striking and successful designs are those that break with convention.

This garden combines pretty and tasty, mixing flowers with food crops in a spirited design that blurs the line between edible and ornamental.

It's a practical solution when you lack space for vegetables. A mixed garden this attractive and tidy could fill an entire backyard and rate rave reviews for viewing and tasting.

When an expanse of lawn becomes more work than it merits, and you'd rather be rewarded with edible crops and splashes of color, construct raised beds and paths. The two rectangular beds shown here are part of a large garden that includes whiskey barrels, trellises, arbors, and other raised beds of various shapes. Throughout, lettuces, small shrubs, johnny-jump-ups, cabbages, and herbs intermingle.

A clay pot partially buried in one bed is a decorative element as well as a practical watering device. When filled, the pot allows water to gradually seep into surrounding soil, moistening the growing medium while conserving water.

This type of garden is ideal for growing flowers for cutting. In traditional ornamental beds and borders, cut flowers leave gaps after they've been harvested. In a garden such as this, with constant harvesting and planting, spaces quickly fill with new plants.

Raised beds are an efficient way to grow food. With structures, such as arbors and tepees, the garden is tidy and easy to access.

PLANT LIST

A. **8 Boxwoods** *(Buxus sempervirens)*: Zones 5–9

B. **21 Johnny-jump-ups** *(Viola tricolor)*: Annual

C. **2 Chards** *(Beta vulgaris cicla)* such as 'Fordhook Giant': Annual

D. **2 Red cabbages** *(Brassica oleracea)* such as 'Ruby Ball': Annual

E. **2 Golden lemon balms** *(Melissa officinalis* 'Aurea'): Zones 4–11

F. **5 Onions** *(Allium cepa)* such as 'Copra': Annual

G. **1 Golden oregano** *(Origanum vulgare* 'Aureum'): Zones 5–11

H. **19 Looseleaf lettuces** *(Lactuca sativa)* such as 'Royal Oak Leaf': Annual

I. **1 Purple bearded iris** *(Iris germanica)* such as 'Hello Darkness': Zones 3–10

J. **2 Broccolis** *(Brassica oleracea)* such as 'Packman': Annual

K. **3 Parsleys** *(Petroselinum crispum)*: Biennial grown as annual

L. **1 Tall delphinium** *(Delphinium elatum* 'Pacific Giant'): Perennial Zones 4–8

M. **15 Carrots** *(Daucus carota sativus)* such as 'Scarlet Nantes': Annual

N. **1 Borage** *(Borago officinalis)*: Annual

O. **10 Pole beans** *(Phaseolus vulgaris)* such as 'Blue Lake Pole': Annual

P. **22 White and yellow johnny-jump-ups** *(Viola tricolor)*: Annual

Q. **6 Heliotropes** *(Heliotropium arborescens)*: Zone 11, annual elsewhere

R. **1 Rhubarb** *(Rheum rhabarbarum)*: Zones 2–9

S. **4 Hot peppers** *(Capsicum annuum)*: Annual

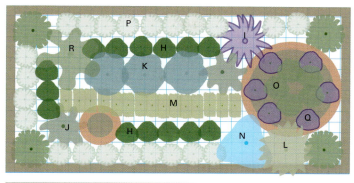

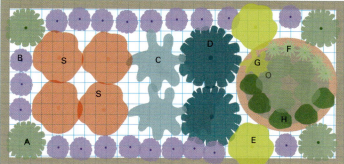

Each square = 6 inches

Herb Garden

A bed of herbs is a living spice cabinet. Just stroll out to the garden before dinner and snip a few herbs to perk up the meal.

Herbs tumble into one another, making efficient use of this small space. The reach from garden's edge to the herbs in the center is convenient at no more than 4 feet. A circle of stones rings the bed, containing garden sprawl and elevating the soil for a raised bed. Nearly all herbs like the good drainage that raised beds provide.

The stone edging absorbs the sun's heat and passes it along to the herbs. Because many herbs are natives of hot, arid climates, they thrive on the reflected heat of the stone edging. A trailing plant, such as woolly thyme, scrambles across the stone surface, keeping the herb leaves high and dry.

Further, most herbs grow best in sandy or gravelly soil, developing intense flavor with minimal nutrients, which is reflective of the poor, rocky soils of arid regions where they originated. Avoid filling the raised bed with moist, rich compost; instead fill it with a sandy soil mix.

The center of the bed has a vertical support, a tuteur (pronounced too-TOOR), which can be purchased premade or built with a few simple materials.

On the tuteur shown here, red cypress vine winds its way through the supports. If you prefer edibles, cherry tomatoes or scarlet runner beans are attractive substitutes.

Enjoy fresh herbs all summer, then pick them to dry to add flavor to meals all winter. Plant a mix of annual and perennial herbs.

PLANT LIST

A.   **3 Basils** *(Ocimum basilicum)*: Annual

B.   **1 Flat-leaf parsley** *(Petroselinum crispum)*: Biennial grown as annual

C.   **2 Curly-leaf parsleys** *(Petroselinum crispum 'Moss Curled')*: Biennial grown as annual

D.   **3 Woolly thymes** *(Thymus pseudolanuginosus)*: Zones 5–8

E.   **3 Chives** *(Allium schoenoprasum)*: Zones 3–9

F.   **4 Red cypress vines** *(Ipomoea quamoclit)*: Annual

G.   **2 Common thymes** *(Thymus vulgaris)*: Zones 5–9

H.   **3 Tricolor sages** *(Salvia officinalis 'Tricolor')*: Zones 5–8

I.   **1 Lemon balm** *(Melissa officinalis)*: Zones 4–11

J.   **1 Rosemary** *(Rosmarinus officinalis)*: Zones 8–10, annual elsewhere

K.   **3 Oreganos** *(Origanum vulgare)*: Zones 5–9

L.   **1 Tarragon** *(Artemisia dracunculus sativa)*: Zones 5–9

M.   **3 Dills** *(Anethum graveolens)*: Annual

Each square = 1 foot

Patio Vegetable Garden

This sun-soaked side patio is a favorite spot for lounging. In place of traditional landscaping, a useful—and beautiful— veggie garden fills the spot.

This small but productive garden is inexpensive and easy to manage. The brick patio surface eliminates any worries of tracking in mud from the garden, and rot-resistant lumber forms an edging for the bricks and keeps the compost and topsoil contained in the garden.

Most of the plants can be sown from seed directly in the soil. A few, such as chives, cardoon, and broccoli, can be purchased as seedlings from a greenhouse or garden center.

The dwarf variety apple tree is a permanent feature that stays small enough to grow in this kitchen garden without shading the other plants. In this garden it's trained as an espalier with branches extending in pairs parallel to the wall to save space while producing abundant fruit.

Lettuces edging the beds fade once the heat of summer arrives. In the large bed heat-loving New Zealand spinach in summer fills the space vacated by the lettuce. Bush beans, peppers, or other warm-season crops can replace the lettuce in the small bed.

Harvest lettuce crops continually while the weather is cool. When the temperatures heat up, the lettuce and greens will bolt.

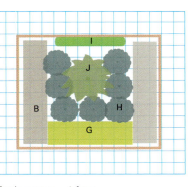

Each square = 1 foot

PLANT LIST

A. **1 Seed packet romaine lettuce** *(Lactuca sativa)* such as 'Winter Density': Annual

B. **2 Seed packets mesclun lettuce** *(Lactuca sativa)* such as 'Salad Bowl': Annual

C. **1 Seed packet New Zealand spinach** *(Tetragonia tetragonioides)*: Zones 9–11, annual elsewhere

D. **1 Seed packet carrots** *(Daucus carota sativa)*: Annual

E. **3 Chives** *(Allium schoenoprasum)*: Zones 3–10

F. **1 Dwarf apple** *(Malus domestica)*: Zones 3–10

G. **1 Seed packet looseleaf lettuce** *(Lactuca sativa)* such as 'Black-seeded Simpson': Annual

H. **7 Broccolis** *(Brassica oleracea)*, such as 'Green Goliath': Annual

I. **5 Pole beans** *(Phaseolus vulgaris)* such as 'Blue Lake Pole': Annual

J. **1 Cardoon** *(Cynara cardunculus)*: Zones 7–11, annual elsewhere

Spring

Mild temperatures make spring the ideal time to grow cool-weather crops. Pack your garden beds with spicy salad greens, plump peas, crisp radishes—and so much more.

Spring Garden

Jumpstart your garden by planning and planting as early as possible.

Spring is the opening act for the gardening season. Seed starting, garden care, and early harvests are spring activities.

Starting seeds

Starting plants from seeds has many practical benefits: You save money, get a head start on the growing season, and choose from varieties beyond those locally available. You also get to experience the joy of watching a seemingly lifeless seed sprout into a living plant. A seed is a plant embryo and its initial food supply is stored within a protective coating. Seeds remain dormant until a combination of moisture, temperature, air, and light triggers germination.

Count backward

Knowing when to start seeds indoors takes some backward thinking. Find out the average date of the last frost in your area and the number of weeks before that date you should start a particular seed. (The number of weeks varies and is listed on seed packages.) Then count backward on the calendar from the average last frost date. As a general rule, start most seeds six to eight weeks before the average last frost date.

Plant creatively and cost-effectively

Use almost anything you want for containers. A cardboard egg carton makes an excellent biodegradable seed-starting flat, as do cut-down milk jugs, yogurt cups, nursery flats, and disposable aluminum pans. Or purchase biodegradable peat pots that can be set in the ground when it's time to move seedlings outdoors. Whatever you choose, make sure the container has holes in the bottom for good drainage.

Seeds are a little fussier about what medium they are started in. Because seeds contain enough food to support the germinating seedlings in their first days, they don't need an especially nutrient-rich medium. Use a sterile, weed-free seed-starting mix that holds water well. Good commercial seed-starting mixtures are available at nurseries and garden centers.

Plant Seeds Outdoors

COOL-SEASON PLANTS, SUCH AS PANSY, CABBAGE, LETTUCE, AND SPINACH, DON'T MIND A BIT OF FROST AND CAN BE PLANTED BEFORE YOUR AREA'S AVERAGE LAST SPRING FROST DATE. BUT HEAT-LOVING TROPICAL VARIETIES, SUCH AS TOMATOES, PEPPERS, AND EGGPLANTS, MAY NOT SPROUT AT ALL UNTIL SOIL TEMPERATURES REACH 70°F OR SO. WAIT TO PLANT THEM UNTIL THE SOIL HAS WARMED.

1 Prepare the seedbed. Loosen the soil by tilling or working it. This makes it easier for seedling roots to grow. If the soil tends to crust or has a high clay or sand content, add a handful of organic matter, such as compost.

2 Sow the seeds just as you would indoors, evenly scattering them over the soil surface. Try not to get them too close together so you don't have to thin them out later.

3 Cover the seeds and water. Cover most seeds with a light layer of soil, compost, or other material to help keep birds and other pests from eating them and to allow the soil to hold moisture better. Water the seeds carefully with a sprinkler or watering can. Try not to apply too much water at once. You don't want your seeds to wash away.

4 Mark seed rows or areas where you've planted seeds so you can easily discern seedlings from any emerging weeds and so you know which varieties are planted where!

Planting Seeds Indoors Step-by-Step

1 GET THE MIX READY
Fill flats or containers with moistened seed-starting mix. Make a spot for the seed using a pencil. Hint: Many peat-based seed-starting mixes repel water when they dry out completely. Moisten the mix by putting some in a container or bag with a small amount of warm water and stirring it well.

2 PLANT SEEDS
Sow seeds into the designated holes. If you have small seeds that are difficult to sow evenly, mix them in a salt shaker filled with sand. Mix them up and shake the seeds out with the sand. Some types of seeds need to be covered by seed-starting mix to sprout. Others will not sprout if they're covered. Check to see whether the seeds have special requirements when you sow them.

3 LABEL THE SEEDS
Stick plant labels in the containers after you sow the seeds to help you keep track of the plants as they begin to grow.

4 WATER
Water softens the seed coat and allows the food source stored within to nourish the emerging seedling. You must keep seed-starting medium moist—but not soggy—until sprouts appear. Small containers dry out quickly, so check them often.

5 MAINTAIN HUMIDITY
Most seeds sprout best in a warm, humid environment. Loosely cover the containers with clear plastic wrap or a clear plastic cover to help hold humidity. Keep the containers out of direct sun; otherwise too much heat may build up and bake the seeds. Don't wrap the plastic cover too tightly; seedlings need fresh air to avoid rot or damping off.

6 SHINE THE RIGHT LIGHT
Seeds vary in the amount of light they need to germinate. Some must have lots of light and should not be covered with soil when sown. Others do best with some light, requiring just a thin covering of soil. Still other seeds germinate best in darkness and should be covered with ¼ inch of fine soil, firmed down. Check the recommendations on the seed packages. After germination, light (natural or artificial) is essential for all seedlings. Seedlings require 12 to 16 hours of light per day. During germination, the warmer the soil, the better.

7 SET OUT SEEDLINGS
As seedlings develop their first set of true leaves (after the initial seed leaves), the containers will become crowded; the plants will need to be thinned. Keep the largest, healthiest seedlings and pull out spindly, less healthy, or crowded plants or cut off stems at soil level, leaving at least an inch between the remaining seedlings. As the survivors grow and outdoor temperatures reach 50°F and above, the seedlings are ready to harden off (get tough) by being set in a protected area outdoors, such as a garage or porch. After a day or two, they're ready for the garden.

Dilled Peas and Almonds

Start to Finish: 35 minutes

2	**cups shelled peas**
¼	**cup sliced onion**
1	**tablespoon butter**
1½	**teaspoons snipped fresh dill**
¼	**teaspoon salt**
¼	**teaspoon black pepper**
3	**tablespoons slivered almonds or broken walnuts, toasted**

Cook peas and onion, covered, in a small amount of boiling salted water for 10 to 12 minutes or until crisp-tender. Drain; return to saucepan. Stir in butter, dill, salt, and pepper; heat through. Sprinkle with almonds. Makes 4 servings.

Curling tendrils, crisp pods, and sweet seeds— garden peas encapsulate spring.

Succulent Peas

Forget the mushy canned peas you grew up with;

freshly picked peas will add a sweet crunch to any meal. These frost-hardy vegetables are high in protein, iron, and fiber and can be grown almost anywhere that's sunny. It's no wonder small children eagerly pluck the first ripening pea pods from their tangled vines. Even a preschooler's nubby fingers can split open a fleshy pod in a second and neatly use a thumb to launch a string of tender green pearls directly onto the tongue. There's something magical about that gentle pop between the teeth and the flavor of beany sweetness—peas taste like spring, a little sweet and a little grassy.

Green, succulent, and sweet. Garden peas intended for cooking and eating fresh weren't developed until the 1500s. Since then many varieties of fresh peas have appeared, including three of the most common in American gardens—sugar peas, snow peas, and shell peas. Both sugar peas (sometimes called sugar snap peas) and snow peas have tender, stringless edible pods, but the pods of sugar peas are fleshier, sweeter, and remain tasty and tender as the seeds inside mature. The whole pod of a sugar pea is a sweet, crunchy treat, making it one of the kid-friendliest vegetables. Snow peas and the tender tips of their vines are frequent ingredients in stir-fry recipes. That flavorful Asian connection is probably because snow peas adapt better to warm-climate gardens than do sugar peas and shell peas. Gardeners can grow big, meaty green peas (the shell peas common to school lunch trays) as well as the delicate petit pois of French cuisine. Whatever you have in mind, peas grow in similar conditions. So there is no need to choose just one.

Planting & Growing Tips

Plant peas when the soil temperature is at least 45°F. Plant seeds 1 to 1½ inches deep with an inch between seeds.

Plant peas in rows 18 to 24 inches apart for easy harvesting.

Most varieties are self-supporting. For those that aren't, help train tendrils onto a fence or other support.

Harvest shelling peas when the pods are swollen and feel plump.

Peas 101

SITE: Plant peas in a location where they can be protected from midday sun when temperatures are higher than 80°F. Choose a sunny area where legumes (peas and beans) have not been grown in the last 3 years. Peas do best in rich, well-drained soil.

BEDMATES: Interplant peas with corn, tomatoes, garlic, onions, and lettuce.

CARE: Peas are cool-weather crops, but plants can be damaged by a late frost. They tolerate brief periods of temperatures to 25°F, but prolonged exposure will interfere with later development. Flowers drop and vines wither in temperatures warmer than 80°F. All but the most dwarf plants require stakes, trellises, or other supports for the vines to climb.

HOW TO START: Grow from seeds.

HARVEST: English or shelling peas are ready to pick when the pods are fully rounded. Harvest snow peas when the pods are flat and the seeds are small and undeveloped. Pick snap varieties when the pods are plump and the seeds are fully developed.

PESTS AND DISEASES: Peas may be susceptible to leaf spot or scab, blights and rusts, fusarium wilt, powdery mildew, botrytis and other molds, damping off, and mosaic virus. Choose varieties bred for resistance to bacteria and fungi common in your area and rotate legume crops each year to avoid diseases that persist in the soil. Beneficial insects control most aphids and thrips, but you can knock these pests off mature plants with a stream of water from a garden hose. Or use insecticidal soap or neem oil spray if infestations are severe. Use floating row covers on young plants to discourage weevils. Tiny holes in pea pods may indicate an infestation by pea moths. Pick and destroy any yellowing pods and destroy all the plant debris after harvest.

recommended varieties

GREEN PEAS
Green peas, also called English peas, are cultivars grown for shelling:
'DAKOTA' is an early variety ready to harvest in 50 to 55 days.
'CASELOAD' is an extra-sweet shelling pea ready in 55 to 60 days.
'MAESTRO' and **'ECLIPSE'** are good choices for hot southern zones.

SNOW PEAS
Pisum sativum var. *macrocarpon* varieties are grown for their edible pods, called snow peas, which may require stringing.
'OREGON GIANT' is a disease-resistant variety that produces sweet large pods in 60 to 70 days and throughout the summer.
'SUGAR POD2' is a better choice for cool zones, bearing in 60 to 70 days.

SNAP PEAS
Other edible-pod varieties, called snap peas, are harvested after the seeds have filled out.
'SUGAR ANN' is the earliest variety, ready to harvest in 50 to 55 days.
'SUGAR SNAP' produces plump, succulent pods in 60 to 70 days in both cool and hot weather.
'SUPER SUGAR SNAP' is resistant to powdery mildew.

Pea Pod Salad
Start to Finish: 20 minutes

⅓	cup bottled Italian salad dressing
1	tablespoon bottled chili sauce
2	cups fresh sugar snap pea pods, trimmed and halved lengthwise
6	cups baby romaine hearts or torn romaine lettuce
4	radishes, sliced

In a small bowl, whisk together the dressing and chili sauce. Add pea pods and toss to coat. Divide lettuce among 6 salad bowls or plates. Top with pea pods and radishes. Makes 6 side-dish servings.

harvest tip

Try picking and tasting two pods a day. This way you'll be able to test the sweetness and the starchiness in order to get the perfect harvest. Peas should be picked right before cooking to get the sweetest taste.

Lemon-Tarragon Peas

Prep: 5 minutes   Cook: 3 minutes

3½	**cups shelled sweet peas**
1½	**cups whole sugar snap and/or snow pea pods**
1	**tablespoon butter, softened**
4	**teaspoons snipped fresh tarragon**
2	**teaspoons finely shredded lemon peel**
½	**teaspoon freshly cracked black pepper**
	Lemon wedges (optional)
	Tarragon sprigs (optional)

In a medium saucepan cook shelled sweet peas, covered, in ¼ cup boiling lightly salted water for 8 minutes. Add the whole sugar snap peas and cook 3 to 4 minutes more or just until crisp-tender; drain well.

Add butter, snipped tarragon, lemon peel, and pepper to peas. Toss gently until butter is melted. If desired, garnish with lemon wedges and tarragon sprigs. Serve immediately. Makes 6 servings.

Fresh Herb Vinaigrette
Start to Finish: 10 minutes

⅓	cup olive oil or salad oil
⅓	cup white or red wine vinegar
1	tablespoon snipped fresh thyme, oregano, or basil
¼	teaspoon dry mustard or
1	teaspoon Dijon-style mustard
1	clove garlic, minced
⅛	teaspoon black pepper

In a screw-top jar combine all ingredients; cover and shake well. Serve immediately or cover and store in refrigerator up to 3 days. Shake before serving. Makes about ¾ cup.

Love fresh mixed greens? Grow them, then step out the back door to make a salad.

Luscious Lettuce & Greens

Fill your garden with a blend of lettuce for colorful meals.

Looseleaf, butterhead (sometimes called Boston lettuce), and romaine (or cos) are three common lettuce types. Include other greens, such as arugula, mâche, cress, mustard, chicory, and mizuna to create tasty salads.

Garden-fresh lettuce has a sweetness and flavor totally distinct from packaged greens from a supermarket. You just can't beat the freshness factor. Crisp leaf lettuce, succulent head varieties, spicy mesclun, dark-green spinach—there are so many types and tastes of greens.

Greens aren't all green.

Swiss chard offers rainbow red, yellow, and white stems. Radicchio features red leaves. Many lettuces have spots and splashes of color that make them beautiful in a big bowl. Texture is another feature. Curly and flat-leaf varieties make for a varied salad too.

Lettuce greens are a health food—most varieties of lettuce, especially dark green- and red-leafed, are high in vitamins A and C, folate, and nutrients. It's fast too. Growing lettuce from seed packet to table takes only about a month. Extend the harvest season by sowing small patches of lettuce every three weeks until late spring, then again in late summer for fall harvest. Pick heat-tolerant varieties for sowing in late spring. As temperatures climb into summer, spring lettuce plants begin to set seed, which causes leaves to become bitter and inedible. This process, bolting, occurs as night temperatures remain about 70°F. When plants begin to bolt, pull them up and compost them. Swiss chard is a green that grows all summer without bolting. Minimize weeds by planting lettuce tightly, with leaves of individual plants touching. Tight space shades soil and crowds out weeds. If you've never planted lettuces before, look for seeds labeled "leaf" or "loose leaf"—these will give you a wide variety of greens to try for taste. If you're not sure about which varieties your family likes, plant several to experience them all.

Planting & Growing Tips

Sow seeds directly in ground or plant sprouts. Water seeds and sprouts lightly to keep the soil moist and cool but not wet.

Grow lettuce in decorative pots. Three or four 18-inch pots will hold enough for a spring season of salads. Lettuces are so shallow rooted that they will also grow in window boxes.

Use a cold frame to grow lettuces in cold weather— early spring and late fall.

Lettuce & Greens 101

SITE: Lettuce isn't picky about the soil in which it grows. Choose a site with sun to part shade and with loose, fertile soil. Amend the soil with well-rotted manure or compost to enrich it and remove any large dirt clods or rocks that would inhibit growth. Although full sun is best, lettuce will grow in a spot that has at least a half-day of sun.

BEDMATES: Plant lettuce around taller plants such as broccoli or peppers. The lettuce keeps the soil moist, cool, and weed-free. As the taller plants grow, they provide shade for tender lettuce leaves as the days warm up.

CARE: As seedlings grow, thin them so the plants are 4 to 6 inches apart. Eat young plants as you thin them, so stagger thinning by a few days to increase your harvests. For instance, thin leaf lettuces first to 2 inches between plants. As the plants grow and begin to crowd each other, thin them to the final 4-inch spacing.

HOW TO START: Start head lettuce indoors 6 weeks before the last frost date and transplant outdoors 3 weeks before the last frost date. Direct-sow other lettuces in early spring or fall.

HARVEST: Leaves are ready to harvest whenever you think they're large enough. Cut head lettuce about an inch above the lowest leaves. Pick alternate heads in the rows so remaining plants have extra room to grow. Snap individual leaves from the outer edges of loose-leaf and romaine lettuces as soon as the plants are big enough to spare a few leaves. Cut baby lettuce leaf blends or mesclun with scissors about 1 inch above the lowest leaves.

PESTS AND DISEASES: A number of pests will dine happily on your lettuce crop: cutworms, slugs, and aphids. To discourage cutworms, use a paper collar around young lettuce seedlings. Repel slugs with a sprinkling of wood ashes or diatomaceous earth on the soil around the plants; reapply after each rainfall. Look for aphids on the underside of tender leaves or hidden inside the crown of the plants. Use insecticidal soap to control. The disease lettuce rot attacks the lower leaves of plants that touch the soil and can spread throughout the plant. To prevent it and other fungal and bacterial diseases, rotate lettuce crops.

guide to greens

Lettuce, the queen of greens, can use a little company in the garden and in the salad bowl. Here's how to identify and add more greens to your culinary repertoire.

Forellenschluss lettuce

lettuce 'Four Seasons'

Swiss chard 'Bright Lights'

alpine strawberry (*Fragaria vesca*)

mustard greens 'Mizuna'

violet

lettuce 'Little Gem'

nasturtium 'Whirlybird'

lettuce 'Cook's Garden Cutting Mix'

lettuce 'Ice Queen'

radicchio
'Indigo'

kale 'Black
Tuscan'

broadleaf
cress

pak choi

curly parsley
'Krausa'

mustard greens
'Osaka Purple'

ARUGULA, or rocket, is native to the Mediterranean region. When harvested young and tender, this leafy green adds peppery flavor to salads. Mature leaves can be sauteed.

CHERVIL is an herb with close family ties to parsley. Its anise flavor and fernlike leaves add spice to salads.

CLAYTONIA is nicknamed miner's lettuce for the California gold rush miners who ate the vitamin C-rich leaves to prevent scurvy. The juicy, succulent leaves resemble tiny lily pads.

CORN SALAD, also called mâche and lamb's lettuce, grows wild in parts of Europe, North Africa, and Asia. Its pretty rosettes of soft, delicate leaves have a mild, nutty flavor.

CURLY ENDIVE adds a pleasantly bitter flavor and texture to salads. Also known as chicory or frisée, the finely cut leaves contrast with the smooth, succulent leaves of Belgian endive, which are often used as crunchy bases for hors d'oeuvres.

GARDEN CRESS, a land-loving relative of watercress, has a peppery, tangy flavor. Leaves are used as garnishes or added to salads, sandwiches, and soups.

KALE is a loose-head form of cabbage. The curly leaves sweeten in colder temperatures. Colorful, ornamental varieties—flowering kale—are also edible.

MESCLUN, often sold as field or baby greens, is a mixture of young greens such as lettuces, endive, arugula, mizuna, tatsoi, chard, radicchio, and mustard greens.

MIZUNA, one of the many types of mustard greens, is a member of the Brassica family. Its ornamental leaves are sweeter than its cabbage and kale relatives.

PAK CHOI (often spelled bok choy) is a Chinese cabbage that forms ornamental vase-shape heads. The green leaves and white stems are sweet and crunchy, fresh or stir-fried.

RADICCHIO, or red chicory, produces compact round, cabbagelike heads of deep red leaves that have a slightly bitter taste. Individual leaves are often used as a garnish.

SWISS CHARD is highly ornamental with its large leaves and contrasting ribbed veins. Varieties have red, yellow, or orange stalks. Leaves are eaten raw when young; mature leaves can be cooked or sauteed, which takes away the slightly bitter taste.

Chicken Salad with Citrus-Pepper Dressing

Start to Finish: 25 minutes

3	tablespoons olive oil
1	teaspoon finely shredded orange peel
3	tablespoons orange juice
2	tablespoons lemon juice
2	teaspoons snipped fresh lemon thyme
2	cloves garlic, minced
¼	teaspoon salt
⅛	teaspoon freshly ground black pepper
	Dash cayenne pepper
3	cups torn romaine lettuce
1½	cups torn speckled lettuce or baby speckled lettuce
1½	cups torn red leaf lettuce or baby red leaf lettuce
12	ounces cooked chicken, cut into strips, or cooked, peeled, deveined shrimp
	Pansies (optional)
	Lemon thyme sprigs (optional)

For dressing, in a screw-top jar combine olive oil, orange peel, orange juice, lemon juice, snipped thyme, garlic, salt, black pepper, and cayenne pepper.

Cover and shake well. Use immediately or chill up to 3 days. (If chilled, let stand 30 minutes at room temperature; shake well.) In a large bowl, toss together the romaine, speckled lettuce, and red lettuce. Arrange on four salad bowls; top with chicken or shrimp. Drizzle with dressing. If desired, garnish with pansies and lemon thyme sprig. Makes 4 servings.

Gardener's Omelet with Wilted Greens

Start to Finish: 25 minutes

2	slices bacon, chopped
1	teaspoon white wine vinegar
½	teaspoon sugar
½	cup torn sorrel leaves or baby sorrel leaves
½	cup torn red kale leaves or baby kale leaves (stems removed)
¼	cup torn beet leaves (stems removed)
1	teaspoon snipped fresh golden leaf oregano or oregano
2	eggs
2	tablespoons water
⅛	teaspoon salt
1	tablespoon butter
¼	cup quartered cherry tomatoes
1	tablespoon crumbled feta cheese
	Golden leaf oregano sprig (optional)
	Pansies (optional)

For filling: In a small nonstick skillet cook bacon until crisp. Remove from skillet, reserving 1 tablespoon of the drippings, and drain on paper towels; set aside. Stir vinegar and sugar into drippings. Add greens and 1 teaspoon oregano. Toss until greens are wilted, 1 to 2 minutes. Remove greens and liquid from skillet; set aside.

In a bowl combine eggs, water, salt, and ground black pepper. Beat with a fork until combined. Heat the skillet on medium-high until hot and add butter. When butter melts, add egg mixture. Lower heat to medium and stir eggs gently but continuously until mixture resembles small pieces of cooked egg surrounded by liquid. Stop stirring and cook 30 to 60 seconds more. Spoon filling onto one side of omelet, then top with bacon. Fold omelet over filling. Transfer to a plate and top with tomatoes and feta. If desired, garnish with oregano and pansies. Makes 1 serving.

Pasta Primavera with Asparagus
Prep: 10 minutes   Cook: 7 minutes

16	**thin stalks fresh asparagus**
8	**ounces dried fettuccine**
1	**tablespoon olive oil**
2	**teaspoons bottled minced garlic**
¼	**teaspoon freshly ground white pepper**
¼	**cup dry white wine**
¼	**teaspoon salt**
3	**small red, orange, and/or yellow tomatoes, seeded and cut up**
1	**tablespoon butter or margarine**
1	**tablespoon snipped fresh thyme or ¼ cup shredded fresh basil**
	Fresh thyme sprigs (optional)

Snap off and discard woody bases of asparagus; rinse. If desired, scrape off scales. Cut or snap off the tips; set aside. Bias-slice asparagus stalks into 1- to 1½-inch pieces; set aside.

Cook pasta according to package directions. Meanwhile, heat oil in a large skillet on medium heat. Add garlic and pepper; cook and stir for 30 seconds.

Add asparagus stalk pieces, wine, and salt to skillet. Bring to boiling; reduce heat. Cook, uncovered, about 3 minutes or until asparagus is crisp-tender, stirring occasionally. Add tomatoes and asparagus tips; cook, uncovered, for 1 minute more or until the tomatoes are heated through. Remove from heat; stir in butter.

Drain pasta. Add pasta and thyme or basil to vegetables in skillet. Toss gently to combine. If desired, garnish with thyme sprigs. Makes 4 servings.

Crispy, earthy spears are ripe for cutting in early spring.

Sweet Asparagus

It's hard to beat the sweet, nutty flavor of just-picked asparagus.

Roasted, steamed, baked, sauteed, eaten raw—it's all good. This early-spring treat is one of the few perennial vegetable crops. Once you get a patch established, you can enjoy years of delicious harvests with very little work.

Asparagus (*Asparagus officinalis*) has been grown for thousands of years—wild in the countryside and cultivated in home gardens. Growing wild in fields, it's a spring treat for foragers. Grown in the garden, it's a reliable crop that produces juicy spears.

Properly planted and tended asparagus beds produce tender, tasty spears every spring—for decades. One of the few perennial vegetables in American gardens, asparagus grows well in regions—generally Zones 4 to 8—that have cold winter temperatures that allow the plants to go dormant for a few weeks.

In ideal situations asparagus grows fast—up to 10 inches a day—so harvest often as soon as spears begin to show. The first season that you plant, allow asparagus to grow without harvesting. The following spring, harvest spears that are ½ inch in diameter. To help plants become established, harvest only for about two weeks.

Each crown produces spears for 6 to 7 weeks during the spring and early summer. Pick asparagus every 4 to 5 days; as the weather warms, you may be able to harvest spears every day. Then allow the shoots to develop into tall, ferny growth—up to 6 feet tall to allow them to build a strong root system to pump out more asparagus the following year.

Asparagus is delicious and good for you. It is high in folic acid and is a good source of potassium, fiber, vitamin B6, vitamins A and C, and thiamin.

Planting & Growing Tips

1 Plant in deep, rich, well-drained soil with a neutral pH. Dig a trench a foot or so wide and deep. Space rows about 4 feet apart.

2 Spread asparagus root crowns 18 to 24 inches apart on shallow mounds of enriched soil in the trench.

3 Cover the crowns with 2 inches of soil and water well. As shoots appear, add 2 to 3 inches of soil until the bed is level with the surrounding garden.

harvest tip

Cut spears when they are at least 5 inches tall and ½ inch in diameter. Look for closed tips.

Asparagus 101

SITE: Choose a sunny location that you can permanently devote to asparagus. The soil should be light, fertile, and well drained. Plan for future space needs because mature crowns may grow up to 24 inches wide.

BEDMATES: Plant asparagus where it has not grown before.

CARE: Asparagus does well in soil pH slightly higher than 7.0. For a reliable crop that lasts several decades, control weeds in the bed and dress the asparagus rows each autumn or early spring with compost. In spring, apply a balanced fertilizer (10-10-10, 12-12-12, etc.). Water frequently until plants are established and continue to water during hot summer weather. When weeding, shallow-hoe to avoid harming the spears underground. Cut back the ferny foliage in the late fall after the plants have gone dormant.

HOW TO START: When you transplant year-old dormant roots called crowns, you can harvest one year sooner than planting younger crowns or seeds.

HARVEST: Gather asparagus in spring as stalks emerge, using a paring knife to cut just below the soil surface. Check daily; the stalks can grow up to 10 inches a day. Continue harvesting until stalks begin to look spindly.

PESTS AND DISEASES: The fungus fusarium rot can rot stems and crowns. Disinfect seeds and roots with fungicide before planting. Control asparagus rust with a fungicide; apply when you see infection. Asparagus beetles and aphids are insect problems; control them with specifically labeled insecticides.

recommended varieties

'JERSEY GIANT' is the most widely grown variety, and it's more disease-resistant and productive than older varieties. Green spears with purplish tips are all male, so no energy is spent on flowering and seed production.

'UC 157' is a great choice for warm-winter regions. Developed in California, it's better suited to hot, dry conditions.

'PURPLE PASSION' bears purple spears that are sweeter than green ones, but the yield is less. Spears turn green when cooked.

Cooking Asparagus

SELECT asparagus spears that are crisp, straight, and firm with tightly closed buds. Asparagus stalks that are thicker than your thumb may be tough and stringy. Try to select spears that are similar in size so they will cook evenly.

TO STORE asparagus, wrap the base of the bundle in wet paper towels and place in a plastic bag. Refrigerate up to 4 days.

CLEAN asparagus just before using. Begin by snapping off the woody base (starting at the base and working toward the tip, bend the spear until you find a place where it breaks easily; snap off at that point). Rinse the spears. If desired, use a vegetable peeler to remove any scales on the stalks.

Prosciutto-Wrapped Roasted Asparagus
Prep: 20 minutes   Roast: 12 minutes   Oven: 425°F

1½	pounds medium to large fresh asparagus (about 24 spears)
1	tablespoon extra virgin olive oil
⅛	teaspoon salt
⅛	teaspoon freshly ground black pepper
3	tablespoons balsamic vinegar
3	ounces thinly sliced prosciutto, cut into ½- to 1-inch-wide strips

   Preheat oven to 425°F. Snap off and discard woody bases of asparagus; rinse. If desired, scrape off scales. Place asparagus in a 15×10×1-inch baking pan. Drizzle with oil and sprinkle with salt and pepper; toss to coat. Roast for 8 minutes, stirring once. Sprinkle vinegar on asparagus; roast 4 to 5 minutes more or until crisp-tender, stirring once. Cool in pan on a wire rack until easy to handle.

   Wrap 1 or 2 strips of prosciutto around 2 roasted asparagus spears. Repeat with remaining asparagus and prosciutto. (If desired, place bundles on the baking pan and roast for 5 to 6 minutes more or until prosciutto is lightly browned and beginning to look crisp.) Arrange on serving platter. Makes 4 to 6 appetizer servings.

Asparagus and Arugula Salad with Shaved Parmesan

Start to Finish: 30 minutes

- ¼ **cup olive oil**
- 2 **teaspoons finely shredded lemon peel**
- 3 **tablespoons lemon juice**
- ½ **teaspoon sea salt or coarse salt**
- ¼ **teaspoon freshly ground black pepper**
- 1 **pound fresh asparagus spears**
- 2 **tablespoons olive oil**
  Salt and freshly ground black pepper
- 4 **cups arugula and/or spinach**
- 4 **ounces Parmesan cheese, thinly sliced**

For salad dressing: In a jar with a screw-top lid combine the ¼ cup oil, lemon peel and juice, ½ teaspoon salt, and ¼ teaspoon black pepper. Cover and shake well; set aside.

Snap off and discard woody bases of asparagus; rinse. If desired, scrape off scales. Brush lightly with the 2 tablespoons oil. Sprinkle with salt and pepper. Set aside. Clean arugula or spinach and remove excess stems; dry. Set aside.

For a charcoal grill, place asparagus spears perpendicular to wire of grill rack directly over medium coals. Grill, covered, for 4 to 6 minutes or until crisp-tender, turning spears occasionally. (For a gas grill, preheat grill. Reduce heat to medium. Place asparagus on grill rack over heat. Cover and grill as directed.)

While asparagus is warm, toss with arugula and dressing, wilting the arugula. Transfer to a salad bowl; top with Parmesan cheese. Serve immediately. Makes 4 side-dish servings.

Strawberry-Radish Salad

Start to Finish: 35 minutes

1	pint fresh strawberries, hulled and halved or quartered
2	oranges, peeled and sectioned
6	radishes, sliced paper thin
3	green onions, thinly sliced
4	teaspoons lemon juice
1	tablespoon sugar
5	cups mesclun
	No-Fat Lemon Vinaigrette
	Salt (optional)
	Black pepper (optional)

In a medium bowl combine strawberries, orange sections, radishes, green onions, lemon juice, and sugar. Let stand at room temperature for 10 to 15 minutes to allow flavors to blend.

In a large bowl toss the mesclun with the No-Fat Lemon Vinaigrette. If desired, season to taste with salt and pepper. Arrange mesclun mixture on a serving platter. Spoon strawberry mixture on top of mesclun mixture. Makes 4 servings.

No-Fat Lemon Vinaigrette: In a small stainless-steel saucepan combine ⅓ cup finely chopped shallots, ¼ cup dry white wine, 3 tablespoons sugar, 1 tablespoon rice vinegar, and 3 cloves garlic, minced. Stir in 1 teaspoon cornstarch. Cook and stir until mixture is slightly thickened and bubbly. Cook and stir for 1 minute more; cool. Stir in 1 teaspoon finely shredded lemon peel and ¼ cup lemon juice.

Fast-growing root crops offer a rainbow of colors.

Robust
Carrots &
Radishes

Long and slender or golf-ball round, orange, red, white, purple, or yellow

carrots come in so many different fun sizes and colors. Sure, you can grow the traditional large orange carrots, but you can also have fun with many different sizes and colors of available for gardeners to grow from seed.

Carrots (*Daucus carota sativus*) are loaded with vitamin A and beta-carotene, both known as antioxidants and cancer fighters. Use carrots raw in salads, explore their charms in moist carrot cake and muffins, or juice them to make a health food drink. And they are, of course, fabulous in soups and stews and as a side dish. Cooking carrots makes the calcium in them more available, which is another nutritional bonus.

Radishes are early gratification for gardeners. Few vegetables grow as quickly and easily as radishes. In less than a month after planting seeds, these crunchy, peppery roots are ready to serve in salads. Growing radishes with kids is fun because radishes germinate quickly and they are so easy to harvest; plucking these little gems from the earth is a treat.

Small radishes (*Rhaphanus sativus*) are ready to harvest in as little as three weeks from sowing. Large radishes, daikon, or winter radishes require longer—up to 50 to 55 days to mature. Because radishes germinate and grow so quickly, they are ideal to interplant with slow-to-emerge crops such as carrots and parsnips. Radish seedlings actually help companion crops grow better because they break the soil crust for slower-growing root crops. By the time the interplanted carrots or parsnips need more space, the radishes are ready to harvest.

Red radishes have vitamin C and the minerals sulfur, iron, and iodine. Large white daikon radishes are higher in vitamin C than red radishes.

Planting & Growing Tips

Begin harvesting radishes when they are less than an inch in diameter, pulling them to eat until they become spongy or cracked. Plant in spring and again in autumn.

Harvest carrots when they reach the full color for the variety.

Keep harvesting carrots as the weather cools. Keep them in the ground, cutting back foliage, and mulch heavily with straw. Dig them throughout winter or in early spring before new growth starts.

Carrots & Radishes 101

SITE: Choose a sunny location with loose, fertile soil. Rake the soil free of rocks.

BEDMATES: Sow radish seeds together with carrots. Both are early-season crops, but the radishes will be ready for harvest first, leaving room for the carrots to develop fully without the need for thinning. Interplant carrots and radishes with lettuces, beans, peas, tomatoes, and peppers.

CARE: When radish and carrot seedlings are about 2 inches tall, thin the plants.

HOW TO START: Grow carrots and radishes from seeds. Sow in early spring, 2 to 4 weeks before the last frost date. Wet the soil before planting to prevent seeds from blowing away. Sow carrot seeds in raised rows 12 inches apart. Cover seeds with ¼ inch of fine soil. Keep soil lightly moist—use a mister to water to avoid washing away the seeds.

HARVEST: Begin pulling carrots as soon as they develop full color. This thinning process allows the remaining carrots to grow larger without becoming misshaped. For winter storage, wait to harvest until after the tops have been exposed to several frosts. The cold will increase their sweetness. Overwinter carrots in the ground by mulching them heavily with straw. Dig them throughout winter or in early spring before new growth starts.

Harvest radishes as soon as they are large enough to eat. The longer they remain in the ground, the spicier they become. Overmature radishes become woody, roots crack, and plants develop a seed stalk.

PESTS AND DISEASES: Carrots and radishes are easy to grow and are virtually disease- and pest-free. Crop rotation solves most disease problems.

recommended varieties

RADISHES

'CHERRIETTE' is ready to harvest 26 days from planting. The variety grows well either as a spring or a fall crop.

'D'AVIGNON' produces elongated red radishes with a white tip in just 21 days. It is a traditional variety from the south of France.

'FRENCH BREAKFAST' bears white-tipped, scarlet roots that have a sweet, mild flavor. Roots are ready in 23 to 28 days.

'MINOWASE SUMMER CROSS NO. 3' daikon radish is best grown as a fall crop. It produces 8- to 10-inch-long tapered white roots in 55 days from seeding.

'NERO TONDO' winter radish features round black roots with crisp white flesh. The 2- to 4-inch-diameter roots take 50 days to mature.

'WHITE ICICLE' produces 4- to 5-inch tapered white roots. Despite their large size, they have a mild flavor. 35 days.

CARROTS

'DANVERS 126' is a heat-resistant variety with tapered, thin roots 7 to 8 inches long. 75 days.

'IMPERATOR 58' bears sweet, tender roots that grow best in loose soils, where they can grow to 9 inches long. 70 days.

'KURODA' produces large yields. It is good for juicing and storage. 73 days.

'PURPLE HAZE' offers purple skins and can grow up to 12 inches long in sandy soils. It has an orange core, and its color fades with cooking. 70 days.

'RED-CORED CHANTENAY' is an heirloom variety with deep orange color from skin to core. It has wide shoulders that taper to a point. 65 days.

'THUMBELINA' is a small round carrot that's good for growing in heavy soils. This 2-inch-long carrot is good for baking. 60 days.

Caramelized Carrots
Prep: 20 minutes Cook: 22 minutes

2	**pounds whole small carrots, peeled, tops on, and halved lengthwise**
2	**tablespoons olive oil**
¼	**teaspoon salt**
4	**cloves garlic, thinly sliced**
⅔	**cup whipping cream**
⅛	**teaspoon cayenne pepper**

In an extra-large skillet cook carrots, cut sides down, in hot oil. Sprinkle with salt. Cook, covered, for 10 minutes. Uncover. Turn carrots; add garlic. Cover and continue cooking for 10 minutes more or until carrots are tender and both sides are golden brown. During cooking, gently shake skillet occasionally to prevent carrots from sticking. Transfer carrots to serving plate; cover and keep warm.

Add cream and cayenne pepper to skillet. Bring to boiling. Reduce heat; boil gently, uncovered, for 2 to 4 minutes until cream is slightly thickened. Pour over carrots. Serve immediately. Makes 8 (½-cup) servings.

Double-Gingered Orange Carrots
Prep: 10 minutes Cook: 20 minutes

1½	**pounds young carrots with tops**
2	**teaspoons olive oil**
¼	**cup orange juice**
1	**1-inch piece fresh ginger, peeled and shaved or cut in very thin slices**
2	**tablespoons chopped, toasted hazelnuts**
1	**tablespoon chopped crystallized ginger**

Halve carrots lengthwise.

In a nonstick skillet cook carrots in hot olive oil on medium heat for 10 minutes, stirring once. Add orange juice, fresh ginger, and ¼ teaspoon salt; toss to coat. Cook, covered, 6 to 8 minutes or until carrots are tender. Uncover; cook 2 minutes or until liquid is reduced by half.

To serve, sprinkle with nuts and crystallized ginger. Makes 4 servings.

harvest tip
Young root crops are tender and sweet. Pull carrots out of the ground as soon as they are at full color. Harvest radishes young and small for the most tasty ones.

Rigatoni with Broccoli, Beans, and Basil
Start to Finish: 25 minutes

- **8** ounces dried rigatoni (about 3½ cups)
- **2** cups fresh broccoli florets
- **1** 19-ounce can cannellini beans, rinsed and drained
- **2** teaspoons minced garlic
- **¼** cup olive oil
- **¼** cup snipped fresh basil leaves
- **2** slices bread, cut into small cubes
- **¼** teaspoon crushed red pepper
  Snipped fresh basil (optional)

In a Dutch oven cook pasta according to package directions, adding broccoli during the last 5 minutes of cooking. Reserve ¾ cup of the pasta cooking water. Drain pasta and broccoli; return to pan.

Meanwhile, in a large bowl combine beans, garlic, and 3 tablespoons of the oil. Mash about half the bean mixture. Stir in basil, pasta water, and ½ teaspoon salt. Stir into pasta and broccoli in Dutch oven. Cover and keep warm.

For croutons, in a skillet heat remaining oil on medium heat. Add bread cubes and red pepper. Cook and stir 1 to 2 minutes or until crisp. Top pasta with croutons and basil. Makes 4 servings.

Harvest these fast-growing, highly nutritious, and oh-so tasty crops!

Cool-Weather
Broccoli&
Cauliflower

Raw or cooked, broccoli and cauliflower are often served together. With similar growth habits and similar flavors, they are members of the vegetable genus *Brassica,* which includes other leafy lovelies such as Brussels sprouts, cabbage, collard greens, kale, and kohlrabi.

Cauliflower is related to the wild cabbage and grows similarly

to broccoli. Cauliflower (*Brassica oleracea Botrytis* group) has a thick stem with a series of tight flower buds at the top, which is called a curd. While broccoli and cauliflower have large leaves that surround the flowering area at the top of the stem, cauliflower uses the leaves to shade the curd to stay white. To ensure the total whiteness of cauliflower, home gardeners tie the big leaves in place over top of the curd. This protection of the curd is called blanching and keeps the area white because the shade affects the production of chlorophyll. However, there are varieties of nonwhite cauliflowers. You can bite into orange, lime green, or purple cauliflowers, which present beautiful serving possibilities for raw vegetable platters.

Broccoli is also a form of wild cabbage, *Brassica oleracea*. There are two types of broccoli. Sprouting broccoli in the early spring, also known as Italian Broccoli, has loose, leafy stems with no central head. The other type produces a large, dense central flowering head—what you get in grocery stores when you buy a whole broccoli. Each flowering piece is a floret. The head form of broccoli, calabrese, is harvested in summer. The vegetable treat broccoli rabe is not actually a broccoli; it is a member of the Brassica family.

Broccoli and cauliflower always top the list of healthful foods. Broccoli is a good source of vitamin C as well as folate, the naturally occurring form of folic acid that is touted for anti-cancer-producing properties. Cauliflower is also a good source of vitamin C. Eaten raw, steamed, sauteed, roasted, boiled, or baked, both these Brassica family members make tasty and nutritious dishes when they are ready to harvest in summer.

Planting & Growing Tips

Plant seeds indoors ¼ to ½ inch deep in the very early spring, then transplant into the garden. Or plant nursery-purchased seedlings; position a bit deeper than the containers they are grown in.

Tie leaves around cauliflower to keep curd white.

Harvest broccoli and cauliflower with a sharp knife—cut at an angle. For cauliflower types that need blanching, cover the developing head when it is 2 inches in diameter. Harvest the head about 10 days later when it reaches 6 to 8 inches in diameter. For broccoli, harvest while florets are tight and green.

Cauliflower & Broccoli 101

SITE: Broccoli and cauliflower are cool-season crops that require full sun and rich, well-drained soil.

BEDMATES: Broccoli and cauliflower have an upright growth, so they can be planted in rows nearby without shading each other.

CARE: Keep well watered. Hand-weed around seedlings. Thin seedlings to 18 to 14 inches apart.

HOW TO START: Seeds or seedlings. Get a jump on early spring planting by starting seeds indoors.

HARVEST: Sever broccoli heads with a sharp knife when they're tight and firm, before any of the buds open into yellow flowers. The tiny yellow flowers that bloom from the florets indicate that the broccoli is past its peak, although it is still edible. Cut broccoli stems at an angle to reduce the likelihood of the stem rotting; continue to harvest the small side shoots. Once you harvest the head of a cauliflower, pull the plant out of the ground and compost it.

PESTS AND DISEASES: Broccoli and cauliflower, so closely related, share some of the same pests. Tiny aphids can build colonies on the undersides of the leaves—use insecticidal soap to treat. Cabbage worms or cabbage loopers (*below*) are the most common pests, attacking leaves and heads. These smooth green caterpillars can destroy an entire harvest if not controlled. Use Bt to control.

recommended varieties

BROCCOLI
'ARCADIA' is a good disease-resistant variety for areas with foggy or wet conditions. Its tightly packed main head sheds water well and helps prevent rot. 69 days.
'DE CICCO' is an Italian heirloom variety that bears a small main head and produces a steady supply of side shoots all season long. 70 days.
'GREEN GOLIATH' produces an 8-inch-diameter main head good for freezing. 55 days.
'PACKMAN' forms a head in just 52 days and withstands heat better than most broccoli varieties. It adapts well to the South and warm-summer regions.
'SMALL MIRACLE' grows only 1 foot tall and is a good choice for containers or small-space vegetable gardens. 55 days.

CAULIFLOWER
'GRAFFITI HYBRID' features bright purple heads that hold color well even when cooked, especially with a little vinegar added to cooking water to make it acidic. 85 days
'SNOW CROWN HYBRID' is a standard white variety that's early maturing, widely adapted, and easy to grow. 55 days.
'VERONICA HYBRID' is a romanesco-type that produces unique spiky lime green heads with a mild, nutty flavor. 85 days.

Cauliflower Wedges with Lemon Dressing
Start to Finish: 20 minutes

- **2   small heads cauliflower**
- **2   to 3 ounces thinly sliced Serrano ham, cooked ham, or prosciutto**
- **1   ounce Manchego cheese or Jack cheese, thinly sliced or crumbled**
- **¼   cup olive oil or cooking oil**
- **2   tablespoons lemon juice**
- **1   clove garlic, minced**
- **½   teaspoon salt**
- **¼   teaspoon sugar**
- **¼   teaspoon dry mustard**
- **¼   teaspoon freshly ground black pepper**
- **2   tablespoons toasted pine nuts**
- **2   tablespoons capers, drained**

Remove heavy leaves and tough stems from cauliflower; cut into 4 to 6 wedges each. Place cauliflower in a microwave-safe 3-quart casserole. Add ½ cup water. Cook, covered, on high for 7 to 9 minutes or just until tender. Remove with a slotted spoon to serving plates. Top with ham and cheese.

For the dressing, in a screw-top jar combine oil, lemon juice, garlic, salt, sugar, mustard, and pepper. Cover and shake well to combine; drizzle over cauliflower, ham, and cheese. Sprinkle with pine nuts and capers. Makes 4 servings.

Arugula and Roasted Cauliflower Salad

Prep: 30 minutes   Roast: 30 minutes
Oven: 425°F

2   **medium heads cauliflower, cut into bite-size florets (about 10 cups)**
3   **tablespoons extra virgin olive oil**
¾   **teaspoon salt**
¼   **teaspoon black pepper**
2   **tablespoons champagne vinegar or white wine vinegar**
1   **tablespoon Dijon-style mustard**
⅓   **cup extra virgin olive oil**
8   **cups lightly packed arugula**
1   **large red onion, very thinly sliced**
4   **ounces shaved Parmesan cheese**

Preheat oven to 425°F. In a roasting pan combine cauliflower, 3 tablespoons olive oil, ½ teaspoon of the salt and pepper; toss. Roast, uncovered, for 30 to 35 minutes, stirring twice. Remove; cool.

In a small bowl combine vinegar, mustard, and remaining salt. Whisk in the ⅓ cup olive oil until combined. In a serving dish combine cauliflower, arugula, and onion. Add the vinegar mixture; toss gently. Top with shaved Parmesan. Makes 12 servings.

MAKE-AHEAD TIP: Prepare and roast cauliflower. Place the roasted cauliflower in a storage container or plastic bag and seal. Refrigerate up to 8 hours or until ready to serve. Bring to room temperature before combining with greens and onions.

Green Onion Parker House Biscuits

Prep: 10 minutes   Bake: 8 minutes   Oven: 400°F

1	5.2-ounce container Boursin cheese with garlic and herbs
¼	cup sliced green onions
1	12-ounce package (10) refrigerated biscuits
1	egg yolk
1	tablespoon water
2	tablespoons grated Parmesan cheese
	Sliced green onions

Preheat oven to 400°F. Grease a baking sheet; set aside. In a small bowl stir together Boursin cheese and the ¼ cup green onions; set aside.

Unwrap biscuits. Using your fingers, gently split the biscuits horizontally. Place biscuit bottoms on prepared baking sheet. Spread about 1 tablespoon of the cheese mixture on each biscuit bottom. Replace biscuit tops.

In a small bowl use a fork to beat together egg yolk and the water. Brush biscuit tops with egg yolk mixture. Sprinkle with Parmesan cheese and additional sliced green onions. Bake for 8 to 10 minutes or until golden. Serve warm. Makes 10 biscuits.

Plant versatile
scallions and leeks
to flavor many
dishes from spring
through winter.

Spring
Onions

The scallion goes by many names:

spring onion, salad onion, and, perhaps the most common: green onion. An edible member of the *Allium* genus—whose tangy relatives include tender chives, bulbous storage onions, and mild-mannered leeks—this slender onion has a small white bulb with hollow green foliage. Eat both parts of this plant raw or cooked.

Green onions, milder than storage onions, are excellent chopped for soups or strewn over a giant burrito. The mildness of green onions (*Allium fistulosum*) allows them to be served raw. Fresh or cooked, scallions add flavor and color to a variety of dishes.

A versatile spring and fall crop, green onions take about 60 days to grow from seeds. Harvest them once they grow about 1 foot tall or leave them in the ground to grow bigger and to pick over several weeks.

The leek (*Allium porrum*) looks like an overgrown scallion. The bulb is bigger, but not as large as a storage onion. The taste of leeks is sweeter than onions. Plant leeks in the spring (the same time that scallions and storage onions are planted) and they are ready to harvest in late summer or early fall.

Because leeks can tolerate frost, leave them in the ground and use them as you want instead of bringing them indoors for storage. Leeks can be baked, grilled, and used in soups and sauces. They add rich yet subtle flavor to creamy sauces, soups, and stews. They're a must for any food enthusiast's garden. Be sure to wash leeks thoroughly before cooking because the folded leaves capture soil.

Leeks are a source of fiber, iron, and magnesium, as well as vitamins A and C. Leeks are more nutritious than onions.

Planting & Growing Tips

Hand-pull weeds around scallions and leeks to protect their shallow-rooted bulbs.

Plant leeks in the early spring.

Harvest leeks when they are 1 to 2 inches in diameter at the base.

Scallions & Leeks 101

SITE: Plant in a sunny spot in well-drained soil that's rich in organic matter. If you have clay soil, plant bulbs in a raised bed amended with humus

BEDMATES: Plant scallions and leeks with carrots, beets, kohlrabi, strawberries, Brassicas (broccoli, cauliflower, kale), dill, lettuce, and tomatoes.

CARE: Keep the soil around scallions and onions consistently moist but not waterlogged. Take care when weeding around young plants. Hand-weeding is best because scallions and leeks have shallow root systems; cultivating tools may harm bulbs. Sidedress with fertilizer.

HOW TO START: Direct-seed leeks in the garden a month before the last frost date or start them indoors and transplant outside at the time of the average last frost. Mound soil around stems to exclude light and produce long white shanks.

HARVEST: To harvest leeks and green onions, grasp the plant at the top of the bulb and twist the stalks back and forth to loosen them. Then just pop them out of the ground. Cut off the short roots. This frost-hardy plant can be harvested long after many other garden vegetables.

PESTS AND DISEASES: Generally scallions and leeks are fairly pest- and disease-free.

Although they look similar, scallions are thinner and shorter than leeks.

recommended varieties

LEEKS
'GIANT MUSSELBURGH' is a Scottish heirloom variety that produces 2- to 3-inch-thick stems. It is exceptionally cold-tolerant. 100 days. **'KING RICHARD'** is a tall, thin variety that matures just 75 days after transplanting.

SCALLIONS
'EVERGREEN HARDY WHITE' is a perennial to plant in spring or fall. It's ready to harvest about 65 days after a spring planting. **'PARADE'** produces 12- to 16-inch green onions, ready to harvest in about 60 days.

Herbed Leek Gratin

Prep: 20 minutes   Roast: 35 minutes
Oven: 375°F

3	pounds slender leeks
½	cup whipping cream
½	cup chicken broth
2	tablespoons snipped fresh marjoram or 1½ teaspoons dried marjoram, crushed
½	teaspoon salt
½	teaspoon freshly ground black pepper
1½	cups soft French or Italian bread crumbs
3	tablespoons grated Parmesan cheese
3	tablespoons butter, melted
	Fresh marjoram sprigs (optional)

Preheat oven to 375°F. Prepare leeks, leaving pieces 4 to 5 inches long with white and pale green parts. Cut leeks in half lengthwise. Pat dry with paper towels. Arrange leeks, cut sides down, in a greased 2-quart au gratin dish or rectangular baking dish, overlapping leeks as necessary to fit.

For sauce, in a small bowl combine whipping cream and broth; pour sauce over leeks. Sprinkle with half of the marjoram, the salt, and pepper. Cover tightly with foil. Bake for 20 minutes.

Meanwhile, in a small bowl combine bread crumbs, cheese, and remaining marjoram. Drizzle with butter; toss to coat crumbs. Sprinkle leeks with bread crumb mixture. Bake, uncovered, for 15 to 20 minutes more or until leeks are tender and crumbs are golden brown. If desired, garnish with fresh marjoram sprigs. Makes 6 servings.

Dilled Green Onion Cheese Ball

Prep: 35 minutes   Chill: 4 hours
Stand: 15 minutes

1	**8-ounce package cream cheese**
1	**cup finely shredded Gouda cheese (4 ounces)**
¼	**cup butter**
1	**tablespoon milk**
½	**teaspoon Worcestershire sauce for chicken**
2	**tablespoons thinly sliced green onion (1)**
2	**tablespoons snipped fresh dill or 2 teaspoons dried dillweed**
½	**cup chopped toasted almonds**
	Assorted crackers and/or flatbread

In a large mixing bowl let cream cheese, Gouda, and butter stand at room temperature for 30 minutes. Add milk and Worcestershire sauce. Beat on medium until light and fluffy. Stir in green onion and dill. Cover and chill for 4 to 24 hours.

Before serving, shape cheese mixture into a ball. Roll ball in nuts and let stand 15 minutes. Serve with crackers or flatbread. Makes about 30 (1-tablespoon) servings.

MAKE-AHEAD DIRECTIONS: Prepare as above, shaping cheese mixture into a ball; wrap in plastic wrap. Freeze up to 1 month. To serve, thaw the cheese ball in the refrigerator overnight. Unwrap and roll in nuts. Let the cheese ball stand at room temperature for 15 minutes before serving.

PROSCIUTTO-BASIL CHEESE BALL: Prepare as above, except substitute finely shredded fontina cheese for the Gouda cheese; stir in 2 ounces chopped prosciutto and 2 tablespoons snipped fresh basil with the green onion; omit the dill. Substitute chopped toasted pine nuts for the almonds. If desired, serve with apples, crackers, or flatbread.

SPICY TACO CHEESE BALL: Prepare as above, except substitute finely shredded taco cheese for the Gouda cheese, stir in 2 tablespoons bottled chopped jalapeños with the green onion, and omit the dill. Substitute ½ cup crushed corn chips for the almonds.

TO MAKE LOGS: Divide recipe into 4 portions and shape into logs.

Chapter 4

Summer

Hot weather spurs the growth of heat-loving fruits and vegetables. Savor juicy heirloom tomatoes, glistening berries, hot peppers, and shapely squashes.

Summer Garden

Summer is time to harvest the fruits of your labors. It's also time to be vigilant about watering.

When the summer garden pumps out produce—tomatoes, peppers, and the last of the salad greens and cool-weather crops—it's time to care for your plants to ensure they are healthy and strong.

Water

Because most vegetables aren't drought-tolerant, give them a drink during dry spells. The closer your garden is to a source of water, the easier it will be. While most vegetables like a steady supply of moisture, they don't do well standing in water. About an inch of water per week provided by you is usually sufficient when Mother Nature fails to come through. Water when the top inch of soil is dry. For inground crops, that may mean watering once or twice a week; raised beds drain faster and may require watering every other day.

Weed

Competing weeds steal water and nutrients from vegetables, so keep them to a minimum. Prevent weeds from being a problem by yanking them out when they're young. The smaller the weeds are, the easier they are to pull. They are also kept from reproducing. Regularly hoe or hand-fork to lightly cultivate the top inch of soil to discourage weed seedlings.

Feed

Fertilizing crops is critical to maximizing yields. Organic gardeners often find that digging in high-quality compost at planting time is all the vegetables need. Most gardeners, however, are wise to apply a packaged vegetable fertilizer, following directions on the box or bag. Apply only what's recommended because overapplication can decrease yield.

Harvest

This is the reward, so don't be shy about picking produce! Many vegetables can be harvested in stages. Pick leaf lettuce as young as you like. Harvest summer squash and cucumbers when the fruit is just a few inches long. The general rule: If it looks good enough to eat, it probably is.

Ways to water your veggie garden

There are several options for applying water. Your choice will depend on location, the size of garden, need for water conservation, and other factors. Among your choices are drip irrigation, underground sprinklers, and hand-watering.

HAND-WATERING

For seeds and seedling watering, use a sprinkler attachment or watering can with a rose (the spout where the water comes out) with a fine spray. Too much water (or too vigorous a spray) can wash seedlings or seeds out of the ground.

DRIP IRRIGATION

Low-volume irrigation is an efficient method that releases water to plants without runoff. Place an emitter alongside each plant; use manufactured drip collars, or fashion your own with perforated drip tubing. Conventional spray heads direct water onto the foliage, removing spider mites that live on the underside of the leaves. Low-volume minisprays apply water more economically but don't do as good a job in wetting the foliage. On hot summer days container gardens may need watering daily. Don't let planters become a chore; use a drip-irrigation system to keep them moist. A simple drip-irrigation kit from a local garden center or hardware store takes only an hour or two to install. Once it's set up, it waters for the season.

SOAKER HOSE

Avoid hauling a hose and sprinkler around garden beds and borders. Save time, energy, and cash with water-saving soaker hoses. With this permeable device, water slowly seeps through the length of the hose. Lay one in your garden and cover the hose with mulch to prevent moisture loss to evaporation. Then turn on the water. Attach the hose to an automatic timer and watering becomes even easier.

LAY IT ON THICK

Mulch is an efficient way to keep the soil moist and discourage weeds. Apply a 2- to 4-inch layer of mulch on the soil to slow the water evaporation. Just about any mulch will inhibit most weeds and help soil hold moisture during hot and dry weather. Mulches made from organic matter (such as cocoa hulls, shredded bark, or compost) do double duty by improving soil as they decompose. A mulch of clean straw, compost, or plastic can stop weeds around large plants such as tomatoes. Mulching also insulates the ground in winter. As the ground freezes and thaws, it helps prevent plants such as perennial herbs from heaving.

Basic Heirloom Tomato Salad

Prep: 15 minutes   Marinate: 1 hour

½   **cup balsamic vinegar**
¼   **cup extra virgin olive oil**
2   **pounds (about 8) heirloom tomatoes (such as Gold Medal,**
      Italian Heirloom, and Green Zebra), cut into wedges
1   **medium red onion, thinly sliced**
1   **teaspoon Kosher salt or coarse sea salt**
      Freshly ground black pepper
      Thyme and/or oregano sprigs

In a small saucepan on medium heat, bring balsamic vinegar to boiling. Reduce heat and simmer, uncovered, for 10 minutes or until vinegar is reduced to ¼ cup. Set aside to cool.

Whisk together the olive oil and cooled reduced balsamic vinegar.

Layer tomatoes with the sliced onion in a large serving bowl or dish. Sprinkle with salt and pepper. Drizzle with balsamic vinegar mixture. Marinate at room temperature for 1 hour. Top with fresh herbs. Makes 8 servings.

Plant easy-to-grow tomatoes for tasty additions to the summer garden.

Terrific Tomatoes

One of the true treats of the summer garden,

tomatoes are high in vitamins A, C, and K and contain lycopene, a powerful antioxidant. Savor tomatoes (*Lycopersicon esculentum*) warmed by the sun plucked off the vine and eaten raw. Cook them in soups, stews, and sauces. Make them into tomato sauce and ketchup to enjoy later in the season.

There are two types of tomatoes:

determinate and indeterminate. Determinate tomatoes are compact and produce clusters of flowers at the growing tip. The plants set fruit along the stem within 2 to 3 weeks, and the fruits ripen almost simultaneously. These tomatoes produce a heavy crop all at once. Many paste and early-season tomatoes are determinate. Although many paste tomatoes are good eaten fresh, they are most often used for cooking because of the low moisture content. Indeterminate tomatoes continue to grow throughout the season because the terminal end of the stem produces leaves instead of flowers. New flowers appear continuously along the side shoots and bloom as long as growing conditions are favorable, producing a steady supply of tomatoes all season.

Tomatoes became a staple of North American dining tables in the 1880s, their popularity coinciding with seeds becoming commercially available. By the early 20th century, more than 150 named varieties were available as breeders scrambled to develop meatier, juicier fruits. Most supermarket tomatoes today were developed through years of careful cross-pollination to create fruits that can travel long distances while keeping good looks, often at the sacrifice of taste. Unusual colors and sizes were for many years ignored or passed over.

Heirloom tomatoes are nearly as easy to grow as conventional tomatoes. Full sun, ample moisture, and warm weather produce sweet and juicy fruit. Thanks to preservation efforts of generations of tomato lovers, seeds and transplants are easy to find online and through mail-order sources. Add some to your garden and take a bite from the past.

While the origins of many varieties are no longer known, heritage is safely preserved in the taste, color, shape, and texture of the fruit. The taste and unique looks of heirlooms spurred many gardeners to grow the fruits by the bushels. Heirloom tomatoes, like other fruits, vegetables, and flowers tagged with the "heirloom" label, are open-pollinated, meaning wind, insects, or the plants themselves take care of producing the next genetic mutation. The result is offspring that look and, in the case of tomatoes, taste just like their parents.

Planting & Growing Tips

Plant transplants into the garden 2 weeks after the average last-frost date in your area. Promote strong plants and an ample root system by planting deeply. Set plants into the ground up to their first set of leaves.

Stake or cage plants soon after planting to give them support and keep fruit off the ground.

Water plants deeply during extended dry periods. Tomato plants are resourceful and mine for water. Supplemental watering during drought periods helps plants fend off pests and form fruit.

If you don't have room for a full-size garden, grow tomatoes in containers.

Tomatoes 101

SITE: Tomatoes grow best in highly fertile, well-drained, slightly acid soil. Add amendments, such as well-rotted manure or compost, to improve the planting site. Tomato seeds can be sown directly in the soil, but most home gardeners purchase tomato seedlings to jumpstart the growing season. Plant seedlings in a sunny location after the last frost date. Plant 1½ to 2 feet apart for small bush tomatoes and 3 to 4 feet apart for larger types if not staked.

BEDMATES: Grow indeterminate and determinate tomatoes together.

CARE: In hot climates new transplants may need to be shaded until they are established. Protect them from strong or cold winds. Place stakes or cages at planting time to avoid injuring roots later. Train indeterminate plants up stakes or grow them inside stiff wire cages to elevate the foliage for better air circulation as well as to keep fruit off the ground. Remove suckers—side branches that form in the joints where leaves join the stems—and pinch them out just beyond the first two leaves that develop.

HOW TO START: Grow from seeds or plant seedlings.

HARVEST: Begin picking tomatoes when they have reached full variety size and color. Tomatoes continue ripening off the plant. Pick any fruits remaining on the vine when the first autumn frost is predicted.

PESTS AND DISEASES: Tomatoes are susceptible to a wide variety of diseases caused by environmental stress. Grow healthy plants by choosing varieties bred for resistance to disease and tolerance of problems common to your area. The most common disease are anthracnose, early blight, Septoria leaf spot, tobacco mosaic virus, fusarium wilt, and verticillium wilt. Other problems include blossom-end rot, which is caused by moisture extremes; blossom drop caused by temperature extremes; skin cracking caused by hot, rainy periods followed by dry spells; sun scald caused by overexposure to the sun on one side of the fruit; and catfacing, a puckering and scarring at the blossom end of fruit caused by cool weather or herbicides. Use cardboard collars around tomato transplants to discourage cutworms. Handpick and destroy Japanese beetles and hornworms. Control fruitworms and stinkbugs with a labeled insecticide.

'BOX CAR WILLIE'

A prolific producer, 'Box Car Willie' is covered with clusters of round, red ½- to 1-pound fruits. It has robust, old-fashioned tomato flavor and ripens in midseason.

'SOLDACKI'

Outstanding sweet flavor is the calling card of 'Soldacki'. The meaty, 1-pound fruits ripen to deep pink or red. A high-yielding plant, it ripens in midseason

'ROSE' (RUSSIAN ROSE)

An heirloom from the Amish in New Holland, Pennsylvania, 'Rose' has pronounced sweet tomato flavor. The dusty rose fruits are nearly 1 pound and very meaty.

'BEAM'S YELLOW PEAR'

These sweet yellow pear-shape tomatoes are about 1½ inches long and make the perfect garden snack. A great producer, 'Beam's Yellow Pear' is ready for harvest in midseason.

'CHEROKEE PURPLE'

This variety's rich, smoky, sweet taste makes it one of the best purple-skin tomatoes. Expect many clusters of ½-pound-or-less fruits to ripen in midseason.

'AUNT RUBY'S GERMAN GREEN'

A green beefsteak tomato, 'Aunt Ruby's German Green' has spicy-sweet flavor. The 1-pound fruits grow in clusters of two or three and ripen late.

'ITALIAN HEIRLOOM'

Big red fruits weighing 1 pound or more cover this excellent producer in midseason. Rich tomato flavor and large, uniform-shape fruit make 'Italian Heirloom' a great all-purpose variety.

'NYAGOUS'

The silky purple-black skin of 'Nyagous' encloses flavorful purple flesh. This midseason variety has baseball-size fruits.

'GOLD MEDAL'

'Gold Medal' produces large yellow fruits streaked with red. Tremendously sweet with firm flesh, it ripens early in the season.

'BRANDYWINE'

One of the most popular and readily available heirloom tomatoes, 'Brandywine' is beloved for its copious round, red ½-pound fruits. It ripens in midseason.

'DR. WYCHE'S YELLOW'

This yellow tomato has deep, rich flavor that competes with the best red and pink varieties. It produces 1-pound fruits in late midseason.

'DURZBA'

High-yielding 'Durzba' is a problem-free variety adapted for growth in almost all parts of the United States. Deep red globe-shape fruits are blemish-free and pack robust taste. They ripen in late midseason.

'GREEN ZEBRA'

Typically round and olive yellow with deep green stripes when ripe, 'Green Zebra' is slightly bigger than a golf ball. It is tangy and sweet and ripens in midseason.

'MEXICO MIDGET'

A cherry-size tomato, 'Mexico Midget' produces hundreds of fruits from midsummer until frost. Its rich tomato flavor is ideal for salads or for snacking.

outstanding heirlooms

With hundreds of excellent heirloom tomatoes to choose from, you can spend summer after summer trying them all. These are some of the most flavorful, problem-free, and productive varieties.

Tomato and Mint Salad
Start to Finish: 30 minutes

2½	pounds assorted heirloom tomatoes (such as Aunt Ruby's German Green, Durzba, and Dr. Wyche's Yellow)
1	cup small fresh mint or basil leaves
2	tablespoons red wine vinegar
2	tablespoons olive oil
1	clove garlic, minced
1	teaspoon sugar
⅛	teaspoon sea salt
⅛	teaspoon cracked black pepper
	Lettuce leaves (optional)
8	ounces feta cheese
	Sea salt and cracked black pepper

Slice tomatoes. In a large bowl combine tomatoes and mint. In a small bowl whisk together vinegar, oil, garlic, sugar, salt, and pepper. Pour over tomatoes; toss.

To serve, line salad plates with lettuce (if desired). Divide tomatoes among plates. Top with feta. Pass additional sea salt and pepper. Makes 6 servings.

harvest tip
Yellow tomatoes, higher in sugar than red ones, don't keep as well. Eat them right after you pick them.

Heirloom Insalata
Chill: Up to 6 hours

½   **cup olive oil**

¼   **cup balsamic vinegar**

3   **cloves garlic, minced (2 tablespoons)**

¼   **teaspoon salt**

    Dash black pepper

3½   **pounds assorted heirloom tomatoes (such as Brandywine, Soldacki, and/or Nyagous), cored and cut into wedges**

½   **pound Beam's Yellow Pear tomatoes, halved if large**

1   **pound fresh mozzarella bocconcini or fresh mozzarella cheese, sliced ½ inch thick and slices halved***

¼   **cup loosely packed fresh basil leaves**

    Whole basil leaves

For dressing: In a screw-top jar combine the oil, vinegar, garlic, salt, and pepper. Cover and refrigerate up to 1 week. Shake before using.

Up to 6 hours before serving, arrange tomato wedges on a large rimmed platter. Top wedges with the pear tomatoes and mozzarella. Cover and refrigerate. Just before serving sprinkle with basil and drizzle with dressing. Makes 12 servings.

*NOTE: Bocconcini are nuggets of fresh mozzarella packaged in whey or water.

Corn on the Cob with Herb Butter

Start to Finish: 1 hour

1   cup butter or margarine
1   tablespoon each snipped fresh thyme and marjoram or
    2 tablespoons snipped fresh basil
16 to 20 ears of corn

Stir together butter and thyme and marjoram. Cover and refrigerate for at least 1 hour or up to 24 hours before serving to allow flavors to blend.

Remove husks from fresh ears of corn. Scrub with a stiff brush to remove silks; rinse. Cook, covered, in a small amount of lightly salted boiling water (or in enough water to cover) for 5 to 7 minutes or until tender. Serve with herb butter. Makes 16 to 20 servings.

English thyme, French lavender, Thai basil—snip and sample all the flavors of the world from your backyard.

Savory Herbs

Fresh herbs add so much flavor to foods,

yet have so few calories and fat grams. Herb aficionados date back to ancient times, when herbs were revered for healing properties. Called physic gardens, herb gardens were the precursor of today's pharmacies. Look and you'll find many herbal remedies on the shelves of modern pharmacies: echinacea, chamomile, and St. John's wort.

Culinary herbs are also a great way to travel without leaving home.

Herbs reflect food cultures—regional cooks use what grows well and is plentiful regionally. For example, the unique flavor of Mediterranean food relies on herbs that grow well during the long, sunny days and dry climates of Italy, southern France, and Greece. Thyme, rosemary, and oregano are herbal staples in the dishes from these countries.

In addition to creating authentic dishes with fresh herbs, you'll also experience the myriad shades of green, textures, and fragrance of a well-established and easy-to-care-for herb garden. There are many classic herb garden designs—of all sizes. But you don't need a lot of space to grow herbs. Herbs grow as well in containers as in the ground. Many gardeners who have the space to plant a formal herb garden also keep herbs in containers close to the kitchen door to use in cooking or as garnishes.

If you have the space for a full kitchen garden, plant herbs that you and your family love: basil for pesto, rosemary for pizzas, cilantro for salsa, and mint for sorbets. Once you get used to picking fresh herbs to use in the kitchen, you'll be hooked on growing them yourself.

Growing herbs from seeds or cuttings is very economical. Herb plants are sold in nearly every garden center too. Generally herbs enjoy fertile soil and (for most herbs) a sunny site. Frequent harvesting keeps plants lush and productive throughout the growing season. There are annual and perennial herbs, and some herbs can be grown indoors during late fall and winter.

Planting & Growing Tips

PLANTING HERBS IN POTS

Transplant herbs into individual 6-inch pots or large decorative containers that can hold several plants. Create a mini herb garden in a container that is at least 12 inches in diameter. Herbs with Mediterranean origins, such as oregano, thyme, and rosemary, prefer soil on the dry side.

Fill the pot with potting soil. Press the potted herb into the soil to make a planting hole just the right size and depth. Gently slip the young plant out of its nursery pot. Squeeze the root ball to loosen it.

Set the root ball in the planting hole, with the plant at the same level or slightly deeper than it was in its nursery pot. Lightly press the soil around the plant. Fill a larger pot with several plants, repeating the process for each. Water the soil thoroughly. If needed, top with more soil, leaving 1 inch between the top of the soil and the top of the pot to allow for watering.

Herbs 101

SITE: Most herbs grow best in a sunny spot in well-drained soil.

BEDMATES: Herbs grow well with other herbs. Low-growing herbs, such as parsley and thyme, make excellent flowerbed edging plants.

CARE: Go light on fertilizer, using organic sources that supply nutrients slowly. Feeding herbs a steady diet of nutrients robs them of their essential oils—the components that make them so valuable in the kitchen. Herbs develop their most intense flavor when kept on the dry side. Their water needs depend on soil type, weather conditions, and type of herb. For example, you'll need to water plants growing in sandy soils more frequently than those in clay. Plants use more water during hot, windy conditions with low humidity than when the weather is cool, humid, and cloudy. When watering, apply enough water to moisten the root zone at least 6 inches deep. Soaker hoses or drip-irrigation systems are efficient ways to apply water: They avoid wasting water by applying it just to the root zone of the plants and prevent disease by keeping the foliage dry.

HOW TO START: Start from seeds or cuttings or transplant small herb plants directly into the ground or a container. The best time to plant an herb depends on its cold tolerance and the average last frost date in your area. Sow hardy perennial herb seeds outdoors several weeks before the average last frost date. Most tender annual herbs, however, germinate better in warm soil—so wait until after the average last frost date to plant them.

HARVEST: Throughout summer, snip plants regularly to encourage branching and new growth. Harvest successive cuttings whenever you need fresh herbs. Generally cut no more than one-third of the stem length. Exceptions include chives and lavender: When they bloom, harvest the flowering stems at ground level.

grow these herbs

BASIL Sweet basil—the staple of Italian cuisine that tangos with tomatoes and perks up pesto—is highly prized for its aroma and flavor. While common sweet basil has flat green leaves and a minty flavor, other varieties have purplish, reddish, or ruffled leaves.

CHIVES Harvest the slender, hollow leaves close to the ground and use them fresh or frozen to add delicate onion flavor to vegetables, seafood, eggs, and cheese dishes. The lavender-pink flowers add flavor and color to vinegar. This versatile perennial plant is a cousin of garlic chives and garlic.

CILANTRO/CORIANDER A two-in-one herb: The leaves are cilantro and the seeds are coriander. Easy to grow from seed, tender cilantro leaves are ready for harvest in just a few weeks. Hot weather causes cilantro to form seedpods, which can be dried and used as coriander. Sow monthly throughout summer.

DILL, an annual, grows easily from seed in full sun or light shade and quickly reaches 24 to 36 inches tall. Plant dwarf varieties in containers. For best flavor, harvest leaves just before flowers open and use them fresh. Collect seeds as they turn brown. Cut flowers for bouquets.

LAVENDER This fragrant herb has been romanticized through the ages, and today it is a popular fragrance in potpourris, sachets, and soaps. The flowers are lovely in dried arrangements and wreaths. Lavender has an intense floral fragrance when you brush its grayish foliage.

LEMON BALM makes a sweet-smelling garnish and adds flavor to teas, fruit salads, and lemon desserts. Use leaves in fragrant crafts. A hardy perennial, it spreads each year and self-sows readily. Divide plants each spring and cut them back a couple times a year.

LEMON VERBENA The long, slender leaves of this 3-foot-tall tender perennial have a tart, lemony flavor. It's hardy in Zones 8 to 11 only; in colder zones, grow in a pot and bring the plant indoors in the winter. Preserve the foliage by air-drying and use it in tea, cookies, and chicken dishes.

LEMONGRASS This graceful, tender perennial (Zones 9 to 11) has a distinct lemon flavor and the appearance of an ornamental grass. Grow the plant in a container in full sun and bring it indoors over winter. Use fresh or dried leaves in cooking, especially Thai soups, stir-fries, and other favorites.

MARJORAM With its delicate, mild flavor, sweet marjoram ably seasons almost any meat or vegetable dish. It is a versatile and underutilized herb that substitutes for oregano. Grow the tender perennial (Zones 8 to 10) in a pot and bring it indoors over winter. Preserve it by air-drying.

OREGANO The leaves of oregano have a pungent flavor (fresh or dried) that's excellent in Italian cuisine. Choose Greek oregano, grown from cuttings, for the best flavor; it withstands long cooking times. Given full sun and sandy, well-drained soil, this perennial grows to 2 feet tall.

TARRAGON With sweet, aniselike flavor, the fresh or dried leaves of tarragon are best used in vinegars, sauces, soups, and salads.

MINT Gently pinch a fresh leaf of mint. You'll appreciate the herb's potency as it releases its enchanting scent. Purchase mints grown from cuttings or allow shoots to root in water or damp soil. Seed-grown mints lack leaf flavor and typically don't grow true to species.

PARSLEY With its high chlorophyll content, parsley has long been hailed for its natural breath-freshening qualities, especially after consuming garlic or alcohol. There are two types of parsley: curly-leaf (most often used as a garnish) and flat-leaf (or Italian). Both are high in vitamin C.

ROSEMARY Beautiful in the garden or in containers, rosemary is a tender perennial (Zones 8 to 10) that grows as a medium-size shrub from 2 to 5 feet tall. Prostrate, sprawling forms make good groundcovers or draperies for walls. Rosemary is indigenous to the Mediterranean basin, where it thrives on sandy, even rocky, shores that are misted by heavy dew.

SAGE is a popular culinary herb with a slight lemony flavor when fresh; it has a stronger, mustier flavor when dried. Unlike that of most herbs, the flavor of sage becomes stronger and sharper as it dries. Grow sage easily from seed or start with nursery-grown seedlings.

THYME has dozens of flavors, colors, and plant forms. Sow seeds or start with cuttings. Thyme is said to aid the growth of eggplant, tomatoes, and potatoes when planted nearby in the garden. If you wish to attract bees to your garden, plant thyme.

Basil

Chives

Cilantro/Coriander

Dill

Lavender

Lemon Balm

Lemon Verbena

Lemongrass

Marjoram

Oregano

Tarragon

Mint

Parsley

Rosemary

Sage

Thyme

Rosemary and Garlic Smoked Pork Roast

Prep: 15 minutes   Soak: 1 hour   Grill: 1 hour   Stand: 10 minutes

- **4** cups apple or hickory wood chips
- **1** 2- to 3-pound boneless pork top loin roast (single loin)
- **2** tablespoons snipped fresh rosemary
- **1** tablespoon olive oil
- **4** cloves garlic, minced
- **½** teaspoon black pepper
- **¼** teaspoon salt
- **4** sprigs fresh rosemary
- **½** lemon or lime

At least 1 hour before grilling, soak wood chips in enough water to cover. Drain wood chips after soaking.

Trim fat from meat. For rub, combine the snipped rosemary, olive oil, garlic, pepper, and salt. Sprinkle rub evenly over meat; rub in with your fingers. Insert a meat thermometer into the center of meat.

For a charcoal grill, arrange medium-hot coals around a drip pan. Pour 1 inch of water into drip pan. Test for medium-low heat above the pan. (Hold your hand, palm side down, in the place where the meat will cook. Count "one thousand one, one thousand two," etc. Being able to keep your hand there for a count of five is equal to medium-low.) Sprinkle half the wood chips on the coals; sprinkle rosemary sprigs on chips. Place meat on grill rack over drip pan. Cover; grill for 1 to 1¼ hours or until a meat thermometer registers 155°F. Add remaining wood chips halfway through grilling.

For a gas grill, preheat grill. Reduce heat to medium-low. Adjust for indirect cooking following manufacturer's directions. Grill as above, except place meat on a rack in a roasting pan.

Remove meat from grill. Squeeze juice from lemon or lime over meat. Cover with foil; let stand for 10 minutes before carving. Makes 8 to 10 servings.

Lemon-Thyme Cookies

Prep: 35 minutes   Bake: 12 minutes per batch
Oven: 350°F

- ½   **cup butter, softened**
- ¼   **cup granulated sugar**
- 1   **tablespoon snipped fresh thyme**
- 2   **teaspoons finely shredded lemon peel**
- 1   **tablespoon lemon juice**
- ¼   **teaspoon ground cardamom**
- 1¼ **cups all-purpose flour**
- **Coarse sugar or granulated sugar**

Preheat oven to 350°F. Beat the butter in a medium mixing bowl on medium to high for 30 seconds. Add ¼ cup granulated sugar; beat until combined, scraping sides of bowl occasionally. Beat in thyme, lemon peel, lemon juice, and cardamom. Beat in as much of the flour as you can with the mixer. Stir in any remaining flour with a wooden spoon. Knead until smooth; form dough into a ball.

Divide dough into 3 equal portions. Roll each portion in a 6x4½-inch rectangle (about ¼ inch thick) on a lightly floured surface. Cut dough in 1½-inch squares with a scallop-edge pastry wheel. Sprinkle cutouts with coarse sugar. Place cutouts on ungreased cookie sheets.

Bake for 12 to 15 minutes or until edges are just lightly brown. Transfer to wire racks and let cool. Makes 36 cookies.

To store: Place cookies in layers separated by waxed paper in an airtight container; cover. Store at room temperature up to 3 days or freeze up to 3 months. Thaw cookies, if frozen, before serving.

Corn Relish

Prep: 1½ hours   Cook: 12 minutes
Process: 15 minutes

12	to 16 fresh ears of corn
2	cups water
3	cups chopped celery (6 stalks)
1½	cups chopped red sweet peppers (2)
1½	cups chopped green sweet peppers (2)
1	cup chopped onions (2 medium)
2½	cups vinegar
1¾	cups sugar
4	teaspoons dry mustard
2	teaspoons pickling salt
2	teaspoons celery seeds
1	teaspoon ground turmeric
3	tablespoons cornstarch
2	tablespoons water

Remove husks and silks from corn; cut corn from cobs (do not scrape cobs). Measure 8 cups of corn. In a heavy 8- to 10-quart stainless-steel, enamel, or nonstick kettle or pot combine corn and the 2 cups water. Bring to boiling; reduce heat. Simmer, covered, for 4 to 5 minutes or until corn is nearly tender; drain.

In the same kettle combine cooked corn, celery, red and green sweet peppers, and onions. Stir in vinegar, sugar, mustard, pickling salt, celery seeds, and turmeric. Bring to boiling. Boil gently, uncovered, for 5 minutes, stirring occasionally. Stir together cornstarch and the 2 tablespoons water; add to corn mixture. Cook and stir until slightly thickened and bubbly; cook and stir for 2 minutes more.

Ladle hot relish into hot, sterilized pint canning jars, leaving a ½-inch headspace. Wipe jar rims; adjust lids. Process filled jars in a boiling-water canner for 15 minutes (start timing when water returns to boiling). Remove the jars from canner; cool on wire racks. Makes 15 pints (70 servings).

Pull the husk from an ear of sweet corn to reveal uniform kernels lined up like a smile.

Sweet Corn

Sweet corn and summer are synonymous.

It's hard to imagine a summer picnic or barbecue without a heaping platter of butter-slathered ears on the center of the table.

Sweet corn (*Zea mays saccharata*) is coveted because of its taste. Because it has a higher sugar content than regular corn, this kernel-packed veggie is a favorite among kids. The sweet factor is the primary reason to grow ears in your backyard because freshly picked sweet corn tastes so much better than that from a stand or market. Sweet corn converts its sugars to starch the very second it's picked; heirloom varieties are especially quick to lose sweetness, so pick and prepare them immediately. Then bite into corn raw, boiled, steamed, grilled, or roasted.

Sweet corn is an ancient vegetable,

dating back nearly 10,000 years. It's also the tallest vegetable in the garden, growing more than 6 feet tall. This fast-growing plant (it's actually a grass) usually produces one ear per stalk; but in the best conditions, it produces a second ear. Sweet corn varieties come with white, yellow, or bicolor kernels.

Sweet corn, although easy to grow, does take space. Plant a 10x10-foot plot to ensure proper pollination. With corn, planting more is better because you'll get bigger harvests as well as higher-quality ears. Sweet corn is wind pollinated and needs multiple plants for optimal production. An efficient way to plant corn is in blocks of short rows rather than long rows. Even in small areas, you can grow sweet corn successfully. Small corn varieties grow well in compact gardens—and you can even grow sweet corn in containers.

If you and your family love sweet corn, plan for a continuous supply throughout the summer by stagger-planting varieties a couple weeks apart. Plant a mix of early-, mid-, and late-season varieties for the longest harvest season.

Planting & Growing Tips

Sow seeds in the ground once the soil has warmed up. Space seeds 8 to 12 inches apart.

Plant corn in blocks of three or more plants instead of in rows—this helps provide support for the stalks and helps with pollination.

Remove weeds by hand or hoe shallowly to avoid damaging the close-to-the-surface roots.

Water during drought times to help ear development.

Carefully peel back the husk to check for kernel ripeness.

Sweet Corn 101

SITE: Corn needs a planting location that receives full sun. Soil should have good drainage.

BEDMATES: Underplant corn stalks with pumpkins and beans to save room in your garden. Don't plant different varieties of corn next to each other; they will pollinate each other. Rotate corn crops every year.

CARE: Corn loves good soil—and is a heavy feeder. To fertilize sweet corn plants, use high-nitrogen fertilizer mixes. Sidedress with 33-0-0 plant food. Add nutrients naturally by using compost or manure.

HOW TO START: Start seeds 6 to 8 weeks before your average last frost date. Don't start too early—if seedlings grow inside too long, they may be too weak by transplant time. Use fresh seed every year. Yellow and white corn varieties can cross-pollinate, which may turn white corn to yellow.

HARVEST: With a sharp downward twist, break the shank or stem below the ear without breaking the parent stalk. Cook and eat the ears immediately or prepare them for freezing or canning as soon as possible to retain maximum sweetness. To preserve the sweetness of sweet corn, refrigerate the ears after picking.

PESTS AND DISEASES: Sweet corn can be affected by leaf blight, corn smut, and bacterial wilt; choose varieties that are resistant to specific diseases that occur in your garden. Flea beetles can cause bacterial wilt; protect young plants using floating row covers. Control earworm on early and midseason varieties with insecticide spray. As ears mature they may be attractive to hungry raccoons or deer. A fence around your corn plot will deter these thieves.

harvest tip

When the silks of the ear begin to turn brown at the tips, peel back some of the husk to check for maturity. Perfect sweet corn kernels should be milky. Immature kernels are watery. When sweet corn is past maturity, kernels are tough and doughy.

recommended varieties

Choose from standard sugary (SU), sugar-enhanced (SE), and supersweet (Sh2) varieties with yellow, white, or bicolor kernels. SU is the least sweet but full of rich flavor and offers high yields. Sh2 features two to three times the sugar, but plants are less vigorous than other hybrids. SE offers the highest sugar content and best tenderness but is not as stress-tolerant as SU varieties.

'SILVER QUEEN' is a white standard sugary variety that's a longtime favorite. It matures in 92 days.

'ILLINI XTRA SWEET' is a yellow supersweet variety that matures in 85 days. It freezes well.

'PEACHES 'N CREAM' Hybrid is a bicolor, sugar-enhanced variety that produces small, creamy, tender kernels. Matures in just 70 days.

'BONUS' Hybrid is a baby-type corn that produces three to six small ears on each stalk just 35 days after planting. Use baby corn in Asian dishes.

'GOLDEN MIDGET' is ideal for small gardens. Stalks are 3 feet tall. Four-inch ears are ready to eat in 60 days.

'GOLD BANTAM' is a yellow heirloom variety known for sweetness. Cook within several hours of harvest for the best flavor.

'MANDAN RED FLOUR' has 6-inch ears with pale yellow kernels that mature to deep red when dry. It is a good variety for cornmeal.

Grilled Corn on the Cob
Prep: 10 minutes   Stand: 1 hour   Grill: 25 minutes

- **6**   **fresh ears of corn**
- **2**   **tablespoons margarine or butter**
- **2**   **teaspoons lemon juice**
- **1**   **teaspoon snipped fresh thyme or ¼ teaspoon dried thyme, crushed**

Peel husks back but do not remove. Using a stiff brush or your fingers, remove silk from corn. Pull husks back up around corn. In a large saucepan or container cover corn (husks on) with cold water. Soak for at least 1 hour. Drain, shaking corn to remove excess water. Cover corn as much as possible with husks. If necessary, tie the tips of the husks together with wet kitchen string.

Grill corn (with husks) on an uncovered grill directly over medium-hot coals about 25 minutes or until tender, turning several times. Carefully remove the husks and strings.

Meanwhile, in a small saucepan combine margarine, lemon juice, and thyme. Heat on the grill or stovetop until margarine is melted. Brush mixture over the corn before serving. Makes 6 side-dish servings.

Sweet Corn Soup

Prep: 30 minutes   Cool: 10 minutes

- **2   fresh ears of corn**
- **1   tablespoon cooking oil**
- **1   small apple, peeled and chopped (about ⅔ cup)**
- **1   small carrot, chopped (about ⅓ cup)**
- **1   small onion, chopped (about ⅓ cup)**
- **1   clove garlic, minced**
- **2   14-ounce cans reduced-sodium chicken broth**
- **Salt and black pepper**
- **2   limes**
- **2   to 3 tablespoons snipped fresh thyme or parsley**
- **2   tablespoons butter, cut into 6 to 8 pieces and softened (optional)**
- **Bottled hot pepper sauce (optional)**

Remove husks from corn. Scrub corn with a stiff brush to remove silk; rinse. Cut kernels from cobs (should have about 6 cups). In a 4-quart Dutch oven bring 2 quarts lightly salted water to boiling. Add corn; return to boiling. Cook, uncovered, for 1½ minutes, stirring occasionally. Drain well; set aside.

In a large saucepan heat oil on medium heat. Add apple, carrot, onion, and garlic; cook and stir for 3 to 4 minutes or until vegetables are tender but not brown. Add chicken broth. Bring to boiling; reduce heat. Cover and cook 2 minutes more.

Cool vegetable mixture slightly, about 10 minutes. Add half the cooked corn (about 2½ cups). Place vegetable mixture, one-third at a time, in a blender or food processor. Cover and blend or process until nearly smooth; return to large saucepan. Add remaining corn; heat through. Season to taste with salt and pepper.

Peel and section limes; finely chop sections. Combine lime sections and thyme. To serve, ladle soup into bowls. Top with a pat of butter. Sprinkle with lime-herb mixture. If desired, pass hot pepper sauce. Makes 6 to 8 servings.

TEST KITCHEN TIP: Cut corn from cob by steadying one end on cutting board and slicing downward with a sharp knife.

Chicken Stuffed with Spinach and Sweet Peppers

Prep: 20 minutes   Marinate: 2 hours
Grill: 45 minutes

6	bone-in chicken breast halves (about 3 pounds total)
¼	cup honey mustard
2	tablespoons mayonnaise or salad dressing
1	tablespoon olive oil
1	tablespoon red wine vinegar
2	teaspoons snipped fresh oregano or 1 teaspoon dried oregano, crushed
2	teaspoons snipped fresh basil or 1 teaspoon dried basil, crushed
2	teaspoons snipped fresh rosemary or 1 teaspoon dried rosemary, crushed
1	cup finely shredded mozzarella cheese (4 ounces)
1	cup chopped fresh spinach
½	cup chopped red sweet pepper
3	cloves garlic, minced
¼	teaspoon black pepper

Make a pocket in each chicken breast half by cutting horizontally from one side almost to the opposite side. Place chicken in a resealable plastic bag set in a shallow dish. For marinade: In a small bowl combine mustard, mayonnaise, oil, vinegar, oregano, basil, and rosemary. Pour over chicken. Seal bag; turn to coat chicken. Marinate in the refrigerator for 2 to 4 hours, turning bag occasionally. Remove chicken from marinade, scraping off and discarding excess marinade.

Meanwhile, for stuffing: In a medium bowl combine mozzarella cheese, spinach, sweet pepper, garlic, and black pepper. Divide stuffing among pockets in chicken. If necessary, secure the openings with wooden toothpicks.

For a charcoal grill, arrange medium-hot coals around a drip pan in a grill with a cover. Test for medium heat above pan. Place chicken, bone sides down, on the grill rack over pan. Cover and grill for 45 to 55 minutes or until chicken is no longer pink (170°F), turning once halfway through grilling. (For a gas grill, preheat grill. Reduce heat to medium. Adjust for indirect cooking. Cover and grill as above.) Before serving, discard toothpicks. Makes 6 servings.

Crunchy and sweet or devilishly hot, peppers have something for everyone.

Versatile Peppers

Botanically classified as fruits, peppers

are primarily served as vegetables and seasoning. Chile (or hot) peppers are fruits of the genus *Capsicum*. Usually grown as annuals, peppers are actually perennials that originated in the Amazon basin and have grown in South and Central America since at least 3400 B.C. They were unknown outside the Americas until Christopher Columbus, mistaking them for the unrelated black pepper so prized in the Old World, carried seeds to Spain. From there peppers spread around the globe.

Used in salads, salsas, and sauces,

as well as for roasting, baking, and grilling, peppers are one of the most versatile vegetables in the garden. They are available in a range of heat and flavor levels—from mild sweet peppers to fiery habaneros. They grow in many shapes, including round, oblong, and nearly square. And colors! Peppers can be grown in a rainbow of hues—green, red, yellow, and purple.

Growing peppers is easy. Plant them in the ground or grow them in containers. As tropical hot-weather plants, they worship the heat; always position them in a sunny spot. In addition to culinary peppers, many bright-color ornamental peppers make beautiful container plants.

If you're into peppers for heat (as many people are!), then plant the hottest varieties: Ancho or poblano peppers are mildly hot; jalapeños are several times hotter. Tabasco peppers are up to 50 times hotter and habaneros are 100 times hotter. Pepper heat varies within the same variety—and even the same pod. The heat-producing substance, capsaicin, increases when plants lack water, when pods mature, and when peppers ripen in high temperatures. Capsaicin is concentrated most in pepper ribs, crosswalls, and stems.

Pepper fans reap more than the makings for zesty foods. One crisp, red sweet pepper supplies twice the vitamin A and three times the vitamin C of an orange.

Planting & Growing Tips

Stake young pepper plants to help keep them upright and to give support once they start producing fruit.

Weed around pepper plants using a hoe (or hand-pull) to keep weeds from encroaching and taking soil nutrients and water.

Mulch plants to conserve moisture and control weed germination.

Plant sweet and hot pepper varieties as far apart as possible in the garden to avoid cross-pollination.

Install drip irrigation to make watering easy. Drip systems are also the most efficient way to water.

Pick peppers often to increase yields. Harvest peppers before they mature to keep crops producing fruit. Cut off peppers with scissors or pruning shears to avoid tearing the stems.

harvest tip

When picking and working with hot peppers, use gloves. The oils from extra hot peppers can cause a burning sensation on your skin—and be even more painful if you rub your eyes.

Peppers 101

SITE: Peppers need a sunny location—getting at least 6 hours of sun a day. Because peppers are hot-weather vegetables, choose a location where the temperature is 70 to 75°F in the daytime and no lower than 60°F at night.

HOW TO START: You can start peppers from seeds indoors in late winter and then transplant into the garden after the soil and air have warmed. Start indoors 40 to 60 days before transplanting time. Or you can purchase pepper seedlings.

HARVEST: Most sweet peppers mature in 60 to 90 days; hot peppers take longer to mature—up to 150 days.

PESTS AND DISEASES: Gardeners who use tobacco can spread tobacco mosaic disease to pepper plants; be sure to wash with soap and water before handling pepper plants. Aphids will attack peppers. Look for them on the underside of the leaves and near new growth. Use insecticidal soap to treat.

recommended varieties

SWEET PEPPERS

Sweet peppers are available in a rainbow of colors: green, white, yellow, red, orange, and chocolate brown. All peppers start out green. Left on the plant, they eventually develop color. They are delicious in salads, stir-fries, soups, stews, and roasted or grilled.

'ACE HYBRID' red pepper matures early and grows well in cool climates.

'ADMIRAL' bears blocky fruits that turn from green to yellow at maturity. Matures in 80 days from planting.

'CALIFORNIA WONDER' is a thick-walled sweet pepper used for stuffing. The original variety turns red at maturity, and a yellow form is also available

'CARMEN' produces a sweet bull-horn-type pepper that turns from green to red when ripe, about 75 days from transplanting. A good choice for containers.

'GOLDEN BELL HYBRID' bears 4-inch-diameter deep gold peppers.

'GYPSY' turns pale yellow to orange to red. This early-maturing sweet pepper features elongated fruits.

'SWEET BANANA' gets its name from its mild, sweet flesh and elongated yellow immature form. At maturity it turns red.

HOT PEPPERS

Hot peppers have many different varieties, each with varying degrees of heat. They take up such little space, you can plant several types. They're perfect in containers. The pepper variety determines heat, but the weather also plays a role in flavor. Plants that get less water produce fewer but hotter peppers. And cool, cloudy weather makes peppers less hot.

'ANCHO 211' bears mildly hot heart-shape fruits that are good for stuffing, making chili rellenos, and drying.

'HOLY MOLE' is a mildly hot pepper developed especially for mole sauce. Green fruits mature to chocolate brown.

'PRETTY IN PURPLE' offers attractive purple fruits, stems, and leaves. It's ornamental as well as edible and hot. Fruits turn red at maturity.

'THAI HOT' has pencil-thin fruits borne above the foliage. It offers an attractive display as fruits change from creamy yellow to orange to red at maturity. The extremely hot fruits are used in Thai cooking.

'CAYENNE' bears long, slim, very hot peppers that grow 5 inches long.

'JALAPEÑO' produces dark green, medium-hot peppers. Matures to dark red.

Roasted Peppers

Prep: 25 minutes Bake: 20 minutes
Stand: 1½ hours Oven 425°F

8	large red or green sweet peppers
¼	cup olive oil or salad oil
2	tablespoons lemon juice
½	teaspoon salt

Preheat oven to 425°F. Halve sweet peppers lengthwise. Place peppers, cut sides down, on a foil-lined baking sheet. Bake for 20 to 25 minutes or until skins are blistered and dark. Remove peppers and immediately wrap in foil or place in a clean paper bag. Close tightly and let stand about 30 minutes. Peel peppers, discarding skin, stems, seeds, and membranes. Cut lengthwise into 1-inch-wide strips.

Combine oil, lemon juice, and salt. Pour over peeled, roasted peppers; toss gently. Cover and let stand at room temperature about 1 hour, stirring occasionally. (Or refrigerate several hours or overnight.)

To serve, drain peppers. Arrange on platter. Makes about 2½ cups (ten ¼-cup servings).

Stuffed Peppers Risotto
Start to Finish: 30 minutes

½   **cup uncooked Arborio or long grain white rice**

1¼ **cups reduced-sodium chicken broth**

4   **small or 2 large sweet peppers**
    Salt and black pepper

3   **ounces Parmesan or Romano cheese**

1   **cup 1-inch pieces asparagus or fresh broccoli florets**

1   **cup cubed cooked chicken**

2   **teaspoon snipped fresh tarragon or oregano or ½ teaspoon dried tarragon or oregano, crushed**

¼   **cup whipping cream**

¼   **cup pine nuts or chopped walnuts, toasted if desired**

For filling, in a 2-quart saucepan combine rice and broth; bring to boiling. Reduce heat and simmer, covered, 15 minutes.

Meanwhile, cut tops off small peppers or halve large peppers lengthwise. Remove membranes and seeds. In a 4-quart Dutch oven immerse peppers in boiling water for 3 minutes. Remove; drain, cut sides down, on paper towels. Place in a serving dish, cut sides up. Sprinkle lightly with salt and black pepper; set aside.

With a vegetable peeler, shave 1 ounce of the Parmesan in thin strips; set aside. Finely shred or grate the remaining Parmesan; set aside. Stir asparagus, chicken, and herb into rice. Cover and cook 5 minutes more. Stir in whipping cream, shredded or grated cheese, and nuts. Spoon filling into peppers. Top with shaved cheese. Makes 4 servings.

Zucchini-Olive Couscous
Start to Finish: 30 minutes

2	**cloves garlic, minced**
1	**tablespoon olive oil**
3	**cups chicken broth**
1	**cup pimiento-stuffed green olives, pitted green olives, and/or pitted ripe olives, cut up**
1	**10-ounce package quick-cooking couscous**
3	**medium zucchini, halved lengthwise and thinly sliced (about 3¾ cups)**
2	**teaspoons finely shredded lemon peel**
¼	**teaspoon freshly ground black pepper**
4	**green onions, sliced**
2	**tablespoons snipped fresh parsley**
	Thin strips of lemon peel (optional)
	Lemon wedges

In a large saucepan cook garlic in hot oil for 1 minute, stirring frequently. Add broth and olives; bring to boiling. Stir in couscous, zucchini, shredded lemon peel, and pepper. Cover; remove from heat. Let stand 5 minutes.

To serve, gently stir in green onions and parsley. If desired, top with thin strips of lemon peel. Serve with lemon wedges. Makes 8 side-dish servings.

Get ready
for harvest!
Smoothed-
skinned,
fast-growing
summer
squash is a
big producer.

Summer Squash

Prolific and delicious, summer squash

varieties pump out pound after pound of interesting and sculptural squashes. These beauties can be long, straight, and thin like traditional zucchini. They can feature a swollen base with a thin, bent top like crookneck. They can be shaped like a baseball, such as round zucchini. And they can resemble a flying saucer like a pattypan.

The classic long, narrow, green zucchini is probably the most well-known of the summer squashes. Its smooth skin, meaty flesh, and mild taste make it ideal for kabobs, for casseroles, to stuff and bake, or to grate for moist bread and muffins.

Other summer squashes—crooknecks and pattypan—are multipurpose vegetables: to slice or chop into salads, to add texture and heft to soups (simmer lightly to preserve texture), or to combine with other vegetables.

Summer squash plants are notoriously prolific producers. Only one or two may supply enough for your needs. Before plants start pumping out the goods, you may harvest blossoms for soups or frying. Edible blossoms star in recipes for fried squash blossoms or squash blossom soup.

Summer squash (*Cucurbita pepo*) differs from fall and winter squash. These vegetables are harvested before the rind hardens. (The soft rind can be left on rather than peeled.) In effect, summer squash are harvested before they mature. Because of the early harvest, summer squash are lower in nutritional value than fall or winter squash—they are also higher in water content. That doesn't mean summer squash varieties aren't nutritious; they are a source of fiber and iron as well as many other minerals and vitamins.

Use summer squash for easy summer side dishes. Saute thin-cut rounds or chunks in olive oil and garlic, and then crumble on some fresh oregano. They are also quick grillmates—just slice them into strips, brush them with olive oil, and grill until lightly browned.

Planting & Growing Tips

Use black plastic around the base of plants. Or apply a thick layer of organic mulch around the plants.

Watch for evidence of pests. Squash vine borers burrow into the vines and eat from within.

Pick squash blossoms and eat them—raw or cooked. Female blossoms produce squash fruit, so harvest the male blossoms to eat. Male blossoms have thinner stems than females and are the first flowers produced.

Even a small garden has room for a summer squash plant. A raised bed is the ideal venue for this prolific producer.

Summer Squash 101

SITE: Summer squash need a sunny spot. Because squash spread so much, prepare a site that has a lot of space.

BEDMATES: Plant with beans or corn. Don't plant squash near potatoes.

CARE: If you plant seeds, thin emerging seedlings to three plants per hill. Water squash plants regularly. If possible, use a drip irrigation system.

HOW TO START: Sow seeds (or plant seedlings) 2 to 3 weeks after the last spring frost date. Grow bush types of summer squash in hills 2 to 3 feet apart in rows 3 to 5 feet apart. To plant more intensively (for a smaller space), plant one squash per 4 to 9 square feet.

HARVEST: Check squash vines every day once they start fruiting because squashes grow rapidly—especially in hot temperatures. Use a stick to push back leaves to look for growing squashes; if they escape detection, they can grow too large and are inedible. If you find an overlarge one, harvest it. Summer squash tastes better (and is more tender) if eaten when small. Harvest zucchini and straightneck squash when only a few inches long and pattypans when the size of quarter. Picking produces more squash. Allowing the fruits to ripen on the vine results in less production.

PESTS AND DISEASES: Summer squash varieties are appealing to many insects: borers, cucumber beetles, and squash bugs. One of the most destructive diseases for squash is bacterial wilt, which is carried by cucumber beetles. Watch for this insect and act swiftly. Control them with an insecticide approved for use on vegetables. (Always follow directions precisely.)

recommended varieties

'BLACK BEAUTY' zucchini bears smooth, straight fruits on an open plant. 60 days.

'EARLY PROLIFIC STRAIGHTNECK' is an open-pollinated variety with light cream-color fruits. The neck end is thinner than the blossom end. 48 days.

'EARLY SUMMER CROOKNECK' is an heirloom that has a bent neck and yellow fruits with bumpy skin. Use it as you would zucchini. 53 days.

'GOLD RUSH' zucchini has uniform golden yellow, smooth, straight fruits that are a colorful contrast to green zucchini. 45 days.

'RAVEN HYBRID' zucchini produces dark green fruits in as few as 48 days from planting. The plant is a compact bush.

'SUNBURST' pattypan is a deep golden yellow, flat and round summer squash with scalloped edges. The vigorous plant is quite productive. 50 days.

harvest tip

Zucchini, crookneck, and straightneck summer squashes are best harvested small, about 6 inches long. Pick pattypan or scallop squashes when they are 3 inches in diameter.

Blue Cheese-Stuffed Summer Squash

Start to Finish: 20 minutes   Oven: 400°F

Nonstick cooking spray
4   medium yellow summer squash and/or zucchini
½   of an 8-ounce package reduced-fat cream cheese (Neufchâtel), softened
½   cup shredded carrot
⅓   cup crumbled blue cheese
⅓   cup thinly sliced green onions
⅓   cup fine dry bread crumbs
¼   cup fat-free or light dairy sour cream
⅛   teaspoon black pepper
2   tablespoons chopped walnuts

Preheat oven to 400°F. Coat a 3-quart rectangular baking dish with cooking spray; set aside.

Halve the squash lengthwise. Remove seeds with a spoon, leaving a shell about ¼ inch thick. Place squash halves, cut sides down, in prepared baking dish. Bake, uncovered, for 10 minutes. Turn squash halves cut sides up.

Meanwhile, for filling, in a medium bowl stir together cream cheese, carrot, blue cheese, green onions, ¼ cup of the bread crumbs, the sour cream, and pepper. (The mixture will be stiff.)

Spoon filling evenly into squash halves. Top with walnuts and remaining breadcrumbs. Bake, uncovered, about 10 minutes or until squash is tender and filling is heated through. Makes 8 servings.

Roasted Squash and Pepper Tart
Prep: 25 minutes Roast: 35 minutes Cool: 5 minutes Oven 450°F

> **Nonstick cooking spray**
> 3 **cups cut-up squash, such as pattypan, yellow summer squash, or zucchini**
> 2 **red and/or yellow sweet peppers, cut into wide strips**
> 1 **large sweet onion and/or fennel bulb, cut into wedges**
> 2 **tablespoons olive oil**
> **Sea and freshly ground black pepper**
> 2 **ounces Parmesan cheese**
> ½ **of a 17.3-ounce package frozen puff pastry sheets (1 sheet), thawed**
> ½ **cup halved cherry tomatoes**
> 2 **tablespoons balsamic vinegar**
> 1 **tablespoon snipped fresh thyme**
> 1 **cup purchased refrigerated creamy Parmesan dressing**
> ¼ **cup finely chopped sweet onion**

Preheat oven to 450°F. Coat sides and bottom of 13×9×2-inch baking pan with nonstick cooking spray. Spread squash, sweet peppers, and onion wedges in pan. Toss with olive oil; sprinkle with salt and pepper. Roast, uncovered, 20 to 25 minutes or until tender, stirring once.

Meanwhile, using a vegetable peeler, cut Parmesan cheese into thin strips. Set aside. On a lightly floured surface, roll puff pastry to a 13x9-inch rectangle. Remove baking pan from oven. Add tomatoes to pan. Toss vegetables with balsamic vinegar and half the Parmesan cheese. Spread vegetables evenly in pan. Lay pastry over vegetables, tucking in edges. Return pan to oven; bake for 15 minutes or until pastry is puffed and golden.

Remove pan from oven; cool 5 minutes. Invert a 15×10×1-inch baking pan over pan with pastry. Carefully invert pans together; remove 13×9 pan. Transfer any vegetables that stick to finished tart. Sprinkle tart evenly with remaining cheese and 2 teaspoons of the thyme. In a small bowl stir together dressing, chopped onion, and remaining 1 teaspoon thyme. Cut into squares. Serve tart warm or at room temperature with dressing. Makes 9 servings.

Triple-Green Bean Salad

Prep: 10 minutes   Cook: 5 minutes   Stand: 30 minutes

12 ounces fresh green beans, dry tips trimmed off if desired
2 tablespoons water
⅓ cup fresh parsley, coarsely chopped
4 green onions, sliced (green tops only)
2 stalks celery, cut into ½-inch slices
2 tablespoons olive oil
2 tablespoons lime juice
Smoked sea salt, sea salt, or salt
Lime wedges (optional)

In a 1½- or 2-quart microwave-safe casserole combine green beans and water. Cover and microwave on high for 5 to 7 minutes or just until tender, stirring once after 3 minutes. Drain in a colander. Rinse with cold water; drain again. Transfer to a serving dish. Toss with parsley, green onion tops, celery, oil, and lime juice. Cover and let stand up to 30 minutes.

Sprinkle with sea salt just before serving. If desired, squeeze lime wedges over each serving. Makes 4 to 6 servings.

Snap, green, pole,
bush—beans have
so many varieties
for home gardens.

Bountiful Beans

This crisp green vegetable is as diverse in the garden as on the plate.

Dangling like pendants amid dark foliage, they are dark green, pale yellow, deep purple—even speckled. They range in size from thick pods to long slender pods. The plants range from 2 feet tall for bush types to pole types that may climb to 12 feet. Snap beans, also called green beans, are easy to grow, bothered by few pests. If you choose pole types, they take little square footage in your kitchen garden. Even if you don't have a traditional vegetable garden, you can grow pole beans on fences or other upright support.

Planting & Growing Tips

Plant seeds every 4 inches in rows 2 feet apart for bush types. Plant seeds every 8 inches in rows 3 feet apart for pole types.

To get the longest harvest, plant bush beans at 2- to 3-week intervals throughout the season.

Pole beans need support because they grow vertically. Train beans on trellises or fences or create rustic supports such as branches or tepees.

Cut the terminal end off the top of pole beans to encourage branching.

Thin bean plants to one every 4 to 8 inches.

Weed around the base of pole beans to keep weeds from growing up through the supports.

Pick bean pods every day. Pods taste best when they are small and tender. Pinch or cut off the pods to avoid pulling the plant out of the ground.

Beans can be eaten at various stages of growth. A bean (*Phaseolus vulgaris*) harvested when young, before seeds fully develop, is a snap bean. Once the seeds reach full size but pods have not turned brown, it's a shelling bean. After the pod dries and seeds mature, it's a dried bean.

Beans are as nutritious as they are delicious. Although fresh beans are not as nutritionally powerful as dried beans (which are a protein source), they provide a good source of vitamin C, folate, and iron. Deep green beans also supply beta-carotene.

There are so many ways to prepare beans: Cook them whole, cut them crosswise or diagonally, or serve them French-cut (cut lengthwise). To preserve the natural sweetness of beans, don't cut them at all. Prepare them in your favorite recipes: grilled, steamed, baked, or raw. Beans are a delicious summer dish. And if you have a bumper crop, blanch extras to freeze. Use yellow, purple, and speckled beans raw in salads to showcase their brilliant colors. Once you cook them, they turn green.

Beans 101

SITE: Beans need a sunny spot and warm weather to grow. Locate them in full sun. The soil should be well drained. Add soil enhancements such as composted manure before planting seeds or seedlings.

BEDMATES: Don't plant beans in the same place as other beans or peas. Rotate beds every year.

CARE: Beans grow best where daytime temperatures are warm—70° to 80°F. They can drop blossoms when temperatures go above 85°F. Cold weather will kill them—a frost kills beans and plants may drop blossoms and pods if temperatures dip to 35°F. Otherwise beans are fairly hardy.

HOW TO START: Beans are among the easiest-to-grow vegetables. Sow seeds directly in the ground (after danger of frost has passed). To guarantee a long and varied bean harvest, sow different varieties every 2 weeks.

HARVEST: For a bountiful harvest, pick every day. By picking beans regularly, you ensure the plants keep producing. Harvest most snap beans when pods are 6 to 8 inches long, before pods and seeds reach full size, 45 to 55 days after planting. Specialty bush beans, filet beans, should be harvested when pods are only ¼ inch in diameter. Harvest shelling beans once seeds have reached full size, about 80 days after planting. Dried beans take approximately 100 to 120 days to reach maturity. Because dried pods may split open and drop beans to the ground, place a large pan or bucket under the plants when harvesting dried beans. Harvest lima beans for shelling when the seeds have reached full size and the pods are plump. For dried lima beans, wait until the pods have turned brown and brittle.

PESTS AND DISEASES: Not many insects or diseases go after beans. If you see beetles on plants, handpick them and drop them into a glass of soapy water. Also, crop rotation takes care of most diseases.

recommended varieties

POLE BEANS

'ROMANO' forms a vigorous vine that has pods that remain stringless even when large.
'KENTUCKY BLUE' produces round, 6- to 7-inch-long, sweet-flavored pods. Approximately 60 days to maturity.
'KENTUCKY WONDER' has oval, meaty pods that are stringless when young.
'BLUE LAKE' pole beans are good for eating fresh out of the garden or for freezing or canning. Approximately 64 days to maturity.

BUSH BEANS

'PURPLE QUEEN' is a showy purple bean that turns green after cooking.
'ROSE' offers intense color (marbled red and cream) and great taste for summer salads and soups.
'BLUE LAKE 274' produces 6-inch-long green pods on bushy plants.
'DERBY' produces tender, 7-inch-long pods that are easy to harvest. Plants resist disease well.
'JADE' offers slender, deep green pods that remain tender and productive in the heat of summer.
'ROC D'OR' is a yellow-pod snap bean that's also called wax bean. It bears 6-inch-long yellow pods 52 days after planting.
'ROYAL BURGUNDY' bears nutritious purple pods that turn green when cooked.

LIMA BEANS

'FORDHOOK' lima beans do well even in northern climates. Limas are ready to shell in 85 days or can be harvested in 95 to 100 days for dried butter beans.

Grilled Green Beans

Prep: 5 minutes Grill: 25 minutes

- 12 ounces green beans, trimmed
- 8 unpeeled cloves garlic
- 1 tablespoon water
- 1 teaspoon cooking oil
- 1 or 2 jalapeño peppers, cut into thin strips (do not seed)*
- 2 teaspoons lemon-flavored olive oil (or 1½ teaspoon olive oil and ½ teaspoon lemon juice)
  Salt

In a large bowl toss together beans, garlic, water, cooking oil, and jalapeño strips; set aside. Fold a 36×18-inch piece of heavy foil in half to an 18-inch square. Place bean mixture in center of foil. Bring together 2 opposite edges of foil; seal with a double fold. Fold remaining edges together to enclose the beans, leaving space for steam to build.

For a charcoal grill, place bean packet on the rack of an uncovered grill directly over medium coals. Grill for 20 minutes, turning once. Remove packet from the grill and cool slightly. Carefully open packet (some steam will escape). Return open foil packet to the grill rack. Continue grilling 5 minutes more or just until beans are browned and crisp-tender, stirring occasionally. (For a gas grill, preheat grill. Reduce heat to medium. Place packet on grill rack. Cover and grill beans as above.)

Transfer beans to a serving bowl. Drizzle with lemon-flavored olive oil. Season to taste with salt. To serve, remove peel from garlic cloves, mash lightly, and divide cloves among servings of beans. Makes 4 servings.

*NOTE: Jalapeños contain volatile oils that can burn your skin and eyes. Avoid direct contact with jalapeños as much as possible. When working with all hot peppers, wear plastic or rubber gloves or wash hands immediately after handling.

Pickled Dilled Green Beans

Prep: 45 minutes   Cook: 5 minutes
Process: 5 minutes

- **3   pounds fresh green beans**
- **5   fresh red serrano chiles (optional)**
- **3   cups water**
- **3   cups white wine vinegar**
- **1   tablespoon pickling salt**
- **1   tablespoon sugar**
- **3   tablespoons snipped fresh dill or 1 tablespoon dried dill**
- **½   teaspoon crushed red pepper**
- **6   cloves garlic, sliced**
- **5   small heads fresh dill (optional)**

Wash beans; drain. If desired, trim ends. Place enough water to cover beans in an 8-quart kettle or pot. Bring to boiling. Add beans and, if desired, fresh chiles to the boiling water; return to boiling. Cook, uncovered, for 5 minutes. Drain.

Pack hot beans lengthwise into hot, sterilized pint canning jars, cutting beans to fit if necessary and leaving a ½-inch headspace. Place 1 chile pepper (if using) into each jar so it shows through the glass. Set aside.

In a large saucepan combine the 3 cups water, vinegar, pickling salt, sugar, the 3 tablespoons fresh dill, crushed red pepper, and garlic. Bring to boiling. Pour over beans in jars, leaving a ½-inch headspace. If desired, add small heads of fresh dill to jars. Wipe jar rims; adjust lids. Process filled jars in a boiling-water canner for 5 minutes (start timing when water returns to boil). Remove jars from canner; cool on wire racks. Makes 5 pints.

harvest tip

Harvest beans at any size—it's your preference. Look for firm, crisp pods.

Carrot-Cucumber Gazpacho

Prep: 25 minutes   Chill: 1 hour

- **2   large (about 1 pound) tomatoes, quartered and seeded**
- **1½   cups carrot juice**
- **2   tablespoons coarsely chopped fresh chives**
- **1   medium cucumber, seeded and coarsely chopped (1½ cups)**
- **1½   cups fresh corn kernels (3 ears) (optional)**
- **¼   of a jicama, peeled and chopped (1 cup)**
- **½   cup arugula, shredded**
- **1   to 2 tablespoons prepared horseradish**
- **½   teaspoon salt**
- **4   large or 6 small radishes, quartered or cut into chunks**
  - **Shredded arugula (optional)**
  - **Coarsely chopped radishes (optional)**
  - **Fresh corn (optional)**
  - **Lime wedges (optional)**

In a blender or food processor combine tomatoes, carrot juice, and chives. Cover and blend or process until smooth. Transfer mixture to a large bowl. Stir in cucumber, corn (if desired), jicama, the ½ cup arugula, horseradish, and salt. Cover and refrigerate at least 1 hour or up to 24 hours before serving.

Ladle soup into bowls or glasses. Top with cut-up radishes. If desired, top with additional shredded arugula, radishes, and corn. Pass lime wedges. Makes 5 side-dish servings.

NOTE: The color of the soup will be dark or light depending on the kind of tomatoes used.

Gently curving cucumbers are the perfect vegetable for picklers and picnickers alike.

Crunchy, Cucumbers

Cucumbers are easy to grow and so prolific.

Just one plant produces armloads of crunchy, refreshing fruits. Use cukes to make cooling salads, sandwiches, and appetizers all summer. Add homegrown cucumbers to leafy salads or chopped vegetable salads. Try your hand at pickles. Make jars of super-easy refrigerator pickles or process in a canner, a preserving method that's making a big comeback.

Cucumbers are grouped as slicers or picklers. All slicers are long and thin and are best eaten fresh. Picklers, which are shorter with more pronounced spines or bumps on their skin, are most often preserved as pickles but can be eaten fresh too. Bush varieties produce vines only several feet long and are suited to growing in containers, on trellises, and along fences for efficient use of space. Keep cucumbers watered well to avoid moisture stress, which leads to bitterness.

Cucumbers (*Cucumis sativus*) include several varieties. The best pickling cucumbers, Kirby cucumbers, are small, just a few to several inches long to easily pack into jars. They have firm flesh with few seeds and the skin is thin, which allows brine to penetrate.

Regular, larger garden cucumbers don't work as well for pickling. You can use supermarket English cucumbers, which are long, slender, and wrapped in plastic (though they are prohibitively expensive for large canning projects). Don't use the common waxed cucumber sold at supermarkets; the coating keeps the cucumber fresh longer but interferes with its ability to absorb brine. Test for waxy coating by scraping a thumbnail along the cucumber.

Cucumbers are delicious raw, sliced, or grated into salads and naturals with simple dressings of yogurt or sour cream. Serve with fresh dill or mint for the ultimate simple and fresh side—as cool as a cucumber.

Planting & Growing Tips

Sow seeds outdoors after soil has warmed in spring. Plant seeds ½ inch deep, in groups of 5 or 6 seeds; make rows 6 feet apart.

Use fabric cover over plants to deter cucumber beetles.

Look for cucumber beetles on flowers and leaves; they cause damage to flowers and seedlings by spreading wilt disease. Pick them off and destroy.

Grow cucumbers on trellises or along fences for efficient use of space.

Cucumbers 101

SITE: Plant cucumbers in a sunny spot. Give cucumbers room to spread—they need about 6 feet to grow. In a small garden grow bush varieties, which produce short vines; they are suited to growing in containers, on trellises, and along fences to take up less room.

BEDMATES: Cucumbers enjoy the same growing conditions as beans. Plant cucumbers beneath corn plants to crawl up the stalks.

CARE: Keep cucumbers watered well; if they get too dry they become bitter. To discourage weeds, use black or brown plastic mulch. This also helps plant development because warm, moist soil improves production.

HOW TO START: Sow seeds in the garden after the soil has warmed. Or buy cucumber seedlings and transplant them in the garden after the danger of frost has passed.

HARVEST: Once cucumber fruits set, they develop quickly. Harvest cukes every few days to prevent oversize fruits, which can be bitter and have too many seeds. When harvesting cucumbers, cut them from the vine with scissors or pruners so you don't damage the plant.

PESTS AND DISEASES: Cucumbers are bugged by a few pests: cucumber beetles, aphids, and spider mites. But cucumber beetles cause the most damage, especially to seedlings. Deter cucumber beetles by placing a floating row cover over emerging seedlings to keep moths from laying eggs on the plants. Remove the cover when plants flower so they can be pollinated.

recommended varieties

'BUSH PICKLE' bears 5-inch-long fruits in just 45 days on compact plants. It adapts well to container culture.

'GREEN FINGERS' features tender, smooth-skin, small finger-size fruits with no bitterness. It has a small seed cavity and is highly flavorful. 60 days.

'LEMON' is an heirloom that bears 2- to 3-inch-diameter round yellow fruits that can be used for pickling or slicing. 60 days.

'MARKETER' is an old-time favorite that was an All America Selections winner in 1943. Its 8-inch-long burpless fruits mature in just 45 days.

'SALAD BUSH HYBRID' is an 8-inch-long slicer that grows on a compact plant. 57 days.

'SWEET SUCCESS' develops fruits without pollination for extra yields. It's also disease-resistant and burpless. 54 days.

'TASTY JADE HYBRID' is a vigorous high yielder with 1-foot-long fruits. The plant must be trellised. 54 days.

Cucumber Sandwiches
Start to Finish: 20 minutes

1	cup packed fresh cilantro leaves
½	cup packed fresh mint leaves
1	tablespoon lime juice
1	fresh jalapeño, quartered and, if desired, seeded (see note, page 116)
1	clove garlic, quartered
2	tablespoons grated Parmesan cheese
4	slices whole wheat or white bread
2	tablespoons butter, softened
4	1-ounce slices provolone cheese
½	of a medium cucumber, thinly sliced (1 cup)

In a food processor combine cilantro, mint, lime juice, jalapeño, and garlic. Cover and process until finely chopped. (If you do not have a food processor, finely chop the herbs, jalapeño, and garlic; combine with the lime juice.) Stir in Parmesan cheese.

If desired, remove crusts from bread. Spread 1 side of each bread slice with softened butter. Top 2 of the bread slices with half the cheese. Top with all of the cucumber slices. Carefully top with all of the cilantro mixture, remaining cheese slices, and remaining bread slices, buttered sides down. Cut sandwiches in half. Serve immediately or wrap in plastic wrap and pack with an ice pack or refrigerate up to 4 hours before serving. Makes 2 sandwiches.

Spiky Cucumber Salad

Prep: 20 minutes   Chill: 2 hours

½   **cup rice vinegar**
¼   **cup olive oil**
1   **tablespoon finely shredded lemon peel**
2   **tablespoons lemon juice**
1   **tablespoon grated fresh ginger**
1   **tablespoon sugar**
1½   **teaspoons coarsely ground black pepper**
1   **teaspoon toasted sesame oil**
1   **teaspoon salt**
¼   **teaspoon crushed red pepper**
8   **medium cucumbers**

In a screw-top jar combine vinegar, olive oil, lemon peel and juice, ginger, sugar, black pepper, sesame oil, salt, and crushed red pepper. Close jar; shake well to combine. Set aside.

Cut cucumbers into bite-size strips or sticks. Place cucumbers in a very large bowl. Drizzle dressing over cucumbers; toss to combine. Cover and refrigerate for at least 2 hours or up to 12 hours, tossing occasionally. Drain to serve. Makes 24 to 26 servings.

harvest tip

Harvest picklers when they are 2 to 4 inches long. Start picking slicers when they become 6 to 9 inches long. Some Asian and greenhouse slicing types may grow to 12 inches or longer.

Strawberries with Cream Cheese Filling

Prep: 30 minutes

- 1   8-ounce package cream cheese, softened
- 1   3-ounce package cream cheese, softened
- ½   cup powdered sugar
- ¼   teaspoon almond extract
- 2   tablespoons grated semisweet chocolate (about ½ ounce)
- 32 large strawberries
     Chocolate curls or chocolate shavings (optional)

For filling, in a large mixing bowl beat the cream cheese, powdered sugar, and almond extract until smooth. Stir in the grated chocolate. Set aside.

Cut a thin slice from the stem end of each berry. Stand each berry upright on the flattened end. Cut each berry into 4 wedges, cutting to, but not through, the stem end. Gently pull apart wedges a little and pipe* the filling into the centers of the strawberries, being careful not to pull the wedges completely apart. Serve immediately or cover and chill up to 6 hours. If desired, sprinkle berries with chocolate curls before serving. Makes 32 filled strawberries.

*TIP: To pipe the filling, spoon filling into a piping bag fitted with a large round tip (or into a small resealable plastic bag, seal bag, and snip off a small piece of the plastic bag). Squeeze filling into strawberries.

Harvesting these sweet gems is a treat for kids and adults alike.

Juicy Strawberries

Sun-warmed and sugar-sweet,

fresh-from-the-garden strawberries beat store-bought berries hands down. Strawberries (*Fragaria virginiana*) range in size from tiny alpine strawberries to mammoth varieties the size of a tennis ball. Enjoy fresh berries out of hand or sliced, sugared, and served with milk or cream. Add sliced berries to salads. Make breakfast a gourmet event by tossing a handful of small berries on cereal. Strawberries are excellent in pies and baked goods. They can be juiced or made into jam, jelly, marmalade, and syrup. Add them to ice cream, yogurt, and smoothies. Strawberries top the list of healthful foods because they have hefty amounts of antioxidants. A 1-cup serving of this sweet fruit has 149 percent of the daily requirement for vitamin C, with nary a speck of fat.

Low-growing and bright green, strawberries make an attractive groundcover that also produces a sweet crop. Many gardeners include strawberries as ornamentals in flowerbeds (they make beautiful edging plants). Tucked in a container or hanging basket, strawberries offer snacks to anyone who walks across the patio. The classic strawberry pot holds several plants in one container.

There are three types of strawberries—and they are categorized by when they bear and how they grow: June-bearing, everbearing, and day neutral. For big, juicy berries, plant June-bearing plants. These spring bearers pump out abundant fruit for just a few weeks. For a long harvest season, plant a mix of early, midseason, and late varieties to prolong the sweet feast for more than the 2- to 3-week span that June-bearing berries produce. This strawberry spreads better than other types. Because it sends out lots of runners, it's the best choice for a bed or large planting as it spreads and becomes dense and more productive.

Everbearing strawberries bear lightly all summer long—producing two or three major harvests during the spring, summer, and fall. These plants do not produce many runners. Day neutral strawberries also produce fruit throughout the season. They, too, produce few runners. Both everbearing and day neutral strawberries are good choices for small-space gardens.

Planting & Growing Tips

Plant strawberries in a sunny spot with well-drained soil. Set the plant in the hole and fill in around the roots so the soil just covers the top of the roots.

Grow strawberries in containers. A hanging basket works well or use a strawberry pot; two or three plants fill the top and runners can fill the lower openings.

In early spring, protect strawberry plants against frost. Use row covers to protect from temperatures as low as -25°F.

Remove the blossoms on strawberries the first year to promote root and runner development (and a larger crop of berries the following year).

harvest tip

Berries are ripe when they are full color—regardless of their size. They overripen quickly, so pick often.

Strawberries 101

SITE: Choose a warm, sunny location with good drainage. If you have heavy soil, plant strawberries in raised beds at least 6 inches deep. Space plants 18 to 24 inches apart in rows 2 to 4 feet apart (depending on the size of the strawberry bed). Day neutral types (those that bear fruit regardless of day length) can be planted closer together.

BEDMATES: Do not plant strawberries anywhere that members of the *Solanaceae* crops (tomatoes, peppers, potatoes, and eggplant) have been planted. Also avoid beds that have been previously planted with other berries, melons, or roses.

CARE: Remove runners after first planted. In a few years the plants will have multiple crowns and yields will drop—then you can let runners develop to replace the older plants. Apply a balanced water-soluble plant food as buds develop. Or fertilize with well-rotted manure. After harvest, mow or cut the leaves close to the ground. Mulch in winter.

HOW TO START: Grow from runners.

HARVEST: Begin harvesting most types of strawberries the year after planting—about 14 months from planting in northern zones and 9 months in the South. The highest yields will come from the youngest plants. Pick berries about a month after the plants flower.

PESTS AND DISEASES: Strawberries are susceptible to botrytis fruit rot, leaf spot, and leaf scorch. All can be controlled with adequate drainage and good bed maintenance—and occasional fungicide if needed. Avoid problems by purchasing varieties resistant to disease and plants guaranteed to be disease-free. Aphids and spider mites can be washed off by hard rains or watering. If you use pesticide, don't apply while the plants are blooming or in fruit.

recommended varieties

Some are for dipping. Some are for freezing. Some are delicious piled high on shortcake and smothered with mounds of whipped cream. Each type of strawberry has its own appeal. Why not plant two or three types?

'RUGEN' alpine strawberry bears small white flowers followed by tiny berries all summer. Popular as an edging plant, it forms a tidy clump.

'TRISTAR' is an everbearing strawberry that produces from June until the first frost. It is excellent eaten fresh or frozen.

'STRAWBERRY FESTIVAL' is a firm, long-lasting berry that's delicious in fruit salads.

'CAMINO REAL' is a large strawberry well suited for dipping in chocolate.

'CAMAROSA' berry is red all the way through. It's a sweet berry that's good for cakes and shortcake.

'ALLSTAR' is known for its exceptionally large berries. This June-bearer has good flavor and produces late in June.

'EARLIGLOW' is an early producer with excellent flavor. It has modest yields, and berry size decreases as the season progresses.

'ALBION' is a large, supersweet berry that grows best in cold climates.

Strawberry Delight

Prep: 50 minutes   Bake: 15 minutes   Cool: 2 hours
Chill: up to 24 hours   Oven: 350°F

1¾	cups all-purpose flour
1	cup powdered sugar
¾	cup butter
2	8-ounce packages cream cheese, softened
¼	cup milk
32	or 40 whole strawberries
	Powdered sugar
2½	cups granulated sugar
½	cup cornstarch
2	quarts strawberries
2	cups whipping cream
¼	cup powdered sugar
1	teaspoon vanilla

Preheat oven to 350°F. In a medium bowl combine flour and ¼ cup of the powdered sugar; cut in butter until mixture resembles coarse cornmeal. Press mixture onto the bottom of a 13×9×2-inch baking pan or dish. Bake about 15 minutes or until lightly browned. Cool.

In a large mixing bowl beat the cream cheese, the ¾ cup powdered sugar, and the milk until smooth. Spread on the cooled crust. Hull 16 or 20 of the whole berries and roll in powdered sugar to coat. Evenly space berries on the cream cheese layer, pressing gently. Cover and chill while preparing the strawberry layer.

In a large saucepan combine the granulated sugar and cornstarch. Crush the 2 quarts of berries and add to the sugar mixture. Cook on medium heat, stirring constantly until thickened and clear. Cook and stir 2 minutes more. Remove from the heat and cool. Spread over the top of whole-strawberry layer. Cover and chill up to 24 hours.

To serve, in a large bowl beat the whipping cream, ⅓ cup powdered sugar, and vanilla with a large whisk or electric mixer until soft peaks form. Top each serving with whipped cream and a whole berry. Makes 16 to 20 servings.

The Ultimate Strawberry Truffles

Prep: 30 minutes   Stand: 10 minutes   Chill: 2¾ hours

- **1**   9-ounce package chocolate wafer cookies, finely crushed (2½ cups)
- **½**   cup butter, melted
- **1**   cup whipping cream
- **1**   12-ounce package semisweet chocolate pieces (2 cups)
- **1**   tablespoon strong brewed coffee
- **2**   teaspoons triple sec or other orange liqueur
- **½**   teaspoon vanilla
- **12**   large strawberries with stems, rinsed and patted dry
- **1**   cup strawberries, hulled and cut

In a large bowl combine the chocolate wafer crumbs and the melted butter until well mixed. Press the crumb mixture into the bottoms and sides of twelve 2½-inch muffin cups lined with paper bake cups or twelve 2½-inch silicone muffin cups to make mini pie shells. Set aside.

In a medium saucepan heat cream on medium-low heat just to simmering. Remove from heat. Place chocolate pieces in a medium mixing bowl. Pour cream over chocolate and let stand 10 minutes (do not stir). Add the coffee, triple sec, and vanilla; stir until mixture is creamy. Cover and refrigerate about 45 minutes or until thickened.

Beat chocolate mixture with an electric mixer on medium to high until lightened in color and slightly fluffy. Pipe* or spoon mixture into the crumb shells. Press 1 strawberry with a stem in the center of each truffle. Cover and refrigerate truffles at least 2 hours or until very firm. Place cut strawberries in a blender or food processor. Cover and blend or process until smooth. Cover and refrigerate until ready to use.

To serve, remove truffles from muffin cups and place on a serving platter or dessert plates. Drizzle some of the pureed strawberry sauce on each truffle. Makes 12 servings.

*TIP: Pour chocolate filling into a small resealable plastic bag. Seal bag and snip a small piece off 1 corner. Squeeze the filling into the crumb shells.

Smoked Chicken Salad with Raspberry Vinaigrette
Start to Finish: 20 minutes

⅓   cup balsamic vinegar
⅓   cup seedless raspberry jam
¼   cup olive oil
¾   pound boneless smoked chicken breast*
     or turkey, cut into thin strips
8   cups mesclun or mixed baby greens
2   cups fresh raspberries
¼   cup toasted sliced almonds

For the vinaigrette, combine balsamic vinegar, jam, and olive oil in a screw-top jar; shake well.

Toss chicken with about half the dressing in a large bowl. Line a large platter or bowl with mesclun. Top with chicken mixture, raspberries, and almonds. Pass remaining vinaigrette. Makes 4 servings.

*NOTE: To smoke chicken on a grill, soak 3 cups of wood chips in enough water to cover for at least 1 hour. Brush 4 skinless, boneless chicken breast halves lightly with olive oil and sprinkle with salt and pepper. Arrange medium-hot coals around a drip pan. Test for medium heat above drip pan. Add 1 inch of water to drip pan. Drain wood chips. Sprinkle wood chips over hot coals. Place rack on grill. Place chicken breast halves on grill rack above the drip pan. Close grill hood. Grill for 15 to 18 minutes or until chicken is tender and no longer pink, turning once.

Glistening like gems on the cane, these soft fruits don't last long, so eat them up.

Ripe Raspberries

Enjoy these berries in so many colors.

Red, yellow, purple, or black—you may want to carve out a little room for each. When you plant more than one variety, you can also savor various ripening times and harvests from midsummer through fall. Red and yellow fruits grow one or two crops on stiff, arching canes. Black and purple fruits grow one crop on trailing canes that require trellising.

Raspberries (*Rubus idaeus*) are a special treat—and they taste best picked fresh. This soft fruit does not ship well. (High-quality, organic, store-bought raspberries are expensive.) Yet raspberries are so easy to grow.

Raspberries are fruit-producing powerhouses. Mature red raspberry plants can produce from 1 to 2 pounds of fruit; purple and black raspberries are even more prolific. This plump, seedy fruit grows wild across the United States—sown, in part, by birds who eat berries and deposit seeds in their droppings. Wild raspberries are smaller than cultivated raspberries.

Raspberries prefer sunny spots, although they frequently grow wild in shaded areas. Raspberries, in a range of colors from yellow to red, are hardy in Zones 3 to 9; purple raspberries in Zones 4 to 9; and black raspberries in Zones 5 to 9. Black raspberries tolerate the most heat.

Raspberries are grown by home gardeners for their excellent taste and for eating ripe off the cane. This fruit is a good source of fiber, manganese, and vitamin C—as well as other vitamins. Delicious as well as nutritious, raspberries were used in herbal medicines as far back as 1548.

Planting & Growing Tips

Plant canes in spring in a row with about 2 to 4 feet between plants.

Divide/replant canes in spring or fall to increase patch size. No need to be gentle; use a spade to chop divisions.

Give raspberries a boost at planting time by adding compost or a 10-10-10 fertilizer into the soil.

Prune every year. Each year in early spring, use pruning shears to cut back canes. Pruning raspberries makes healthy, productive plants.

Keep birds away. If birds dip into the harvest, drape netting (sold at garden centers) over the canes. Lift the net to pick them.

Pinch the tips of purple and black raspberry canes in summer to promote branching.

Keep canes off the ground so berries are easy to pick and are unmarred.

Raspberries 101

SITE: Plant raspberries where they will receive full sun. Pick a site with good drainage. In water-retaining clay soils, mound soil into raised beds to keep the canes from developing root rot. Roots like to be moist, not wet, and the plants are healthier with good ventilation.

BEDMATES: Don't plant raspberries in garden beds where tomatoes, potatoes, eggplants, and peppers have recently grown; this soil may harbor verticillium wilt.

CARE: Apply fertilizers in early spring. Make two applications (once in early spring and again in late spring) for fall-bearing plants. In spring remove mature canes and thin new growth. For ease of harvesting and neatness, support on wires stretched between posts. Prune out the current season's fruiting canes immediately after harvesting the summer crop of raspberries. Mulch well with organic materials because raspberries need lots of moisture. Mow the paths between the rows to keep the canes from spreading. Raspberries will spread rapidly by underground runners if not kept in check. Prune the fruiting canes of raspberries in fall. Berries will form on new canes.

HOW TO START: Grow raspberries from root or stem cuttings. Buy bare-root, virus-free plants in early spring. Plant in rows 2 to 4 feet apart. Start raspberries from new suckers or through tip-layering.

HARVEST: Raspberries bear a small crop the second year after planting and a full crop the third year. They are productive for 5 to 8 years, after which they need to be replanted.

PESTS AND DISEASES: A number of fungal diseases, including anthracnose, which is especially hard on black raspberries, attack raspberry plants. Look for small, slightly purple spots that turn gray in the center on the canes. Anthracnose makes canes weak, resulting in small or shriveled fruit. Verticillium wilt affects black raspberries. Lower leaves yellow and drop off. Avoid planting in the same soil as other susceptible crops (potato, tomato, eggplant, pepper, squash, melons, strawberries). Crown gall can stunt and weaken plants. Plant virus-free nursery stock. Insect pests include raspberry cane borer and Japanese beetles, which are ½-inch shiny, metallic green insects that emerge from the soil from June to September. They feed on fruit and leaves. To organically control, handpick and destroy.

recommended varieties

RED RASPBERRIES

'CANBY' produces large, firm berries in midseason. Plants are semi-thornless and do best in well-drained soils in the West and Northwest. Zones 5 to 8.

'HERITAGE' red raspberry bears medium-size sweet, dark red berries in early summer (June) and again in autumn (September). Canes are upright and don't require support. Cold-hardy and does well in poor soils. Zones 3 to 8.

'WILLAMETTE' berries are large, round, and firm. They ripen midseason and are excellent choices for canning and freezing. This vigorous plant is a popular commercial variety and good for the West. Zones 5 to 8.

'MEEKER' produces bright red berries on strong, disease-resistant plants. Zones 4 to 8.

'REVEILLE' bears early-season, sweet-tasting berries. Plants are vigorous and productive. Zones 4 to 8.

'TITAN' produces large, luscious fruits. The plants require well-drained, light soils. Zones 5 to 8.

BLACK RASPBERRIES

'BRISTOL' bears large, firm, glossy black berries for several weeks in summer. This all-purpose raspberry is for eating fresh, freezing, or cooked in jam. Upright canes don't require staking. Pick in early July. Zones 4 to 8.

'JEWEL' is a productive plant. This black raspberry produces a flush of berries in early July—for making into jams or pies. Reliable, hardy, and flavorful. Berries are beautiful black-purple. Zones 3 to 8.

GOLD RASPBERRIES

'FALL GOLD' produces sweet, light-color berries and two crops—one in early summer and again in fall. A good choice for northern gardens. Zones 4 to 8.

PURPLE RASPBERRIES

'ROYALTY' is hardy, vigorous, and resistant to insects and disease. This plant bears large sweet fruit that bursts with flavor. Eat berries fresh off the cane or use in desserts and salads. Easy to grow. Harvest in July. Zones 4 to 7.

Berry Tart

Prep: 30 minutes   Bake: 45 minutes
Oven: 400°F

1	**cup all-purpose flour**
2	**tablespoons sugar**
	Dash salt
½	**cup butter**
1	**tablespoon white vinegar**
2	**cups fresh or frozen raspberries**
2	**cups fresh or frozen blueberries**
½	**cup sugar**
3	**tablespoons all-purpose flour**

Preheat oven to 400°F. For the crust, in a medium bowl combine 1 cup flour, 2 tablespoons sugar, and salt. Using a pastry blender, cut in butter until pieces are peasize. Sprinkle the vinegar over the flour mixture; gently toss with a fork. Form dough into a ball. Press dough mixture evenly in the bottom and up the sides of a 9-inch tart pan with a removable bottom. Set aside.

For the filling, in a large bowl combine raspberries, blueberries, ½ cup sugar, and 3 tablespoons flour. (If using frozen fruit, let mixture stand for 45 minutes or until fruit is partially thawed but still icy.) Transfer filling to pastry-lined tart pan. Bake in a shallow baking pan for 45 to 50 minutes or until fruit is bubbly in the center (if using frozen fruit, bake 50 to 55 minutes). Cool on a wire rack.

harvest tip

Pick in the morning when fruits and plants are dry and cool. Carry the berries in shallow trays because they are easily crushed.

Raspberry Sorbet

Prep: 30 minutes   Chill: 5 hours   Freeze: 20 minutes plus 3 hours

- **1   cup sugar**
- **1   cup water**
- **3   cups fresh raspberries**
- **3   to 5 tablespoons fresh lemon juice**

In a medium-size heavy saucepan combine sugar and water. Cook and stir over medium-high heat until sugar is dissolved and mixture comes to a boil, about 5 minutes. Add raspberries and return to boil; reduce heat. Simmer, uncovered, for 2 minutes, stirring constantly. Press mixture through a fine-mesh sieve into a bowl and discard seeds. Stir in lemon juice. (You should have 2⅓ cups liquid.) Cover and refrigerate 5 to 6 hours or overnight.

Pour mixture into a 1- to 2-quart ice cream freezer and freeze according to the manufacturer's instructions. Transfer to a freezer-safe container and freeze until firm, 3 to 4 hours. Makes 6 servings (about ½ cup each).

NOTE: Even after freezing, this is a soft, creamy sorbet.

Cherry Berry Smoothies

Start to Finish: 15 minutes

- ½ **cup fresh strawberries, hulled**
- 1 **cup pitted dark sweet cherries or 1 cup frozen unsweetened pitted dark sweet cherries**
- 1 **cup fresh raspberries**
- 1 **cup pomegranate juice, chilled**
- ½ **cup fresh blueberries**

In a blender combine strawberries, cherries, raspberries, pomegranate juice, and blueberries. Cover and blend until almost smooth. Makes 4 (8-ounce) servings.

Round, red, juicy, and delicious, cherries star in pies, crisps, and cobblers.

Sweet (& Sour) Cherries

In the early spring, cherry trees burst into a cloud of crepe-paper petalled bloom.

Small fragrant blossoms, on the fasttrack to make fruit, will provide luscious ruby-hue cherries in just 60 days from bloom to picking time.

Cherries are either sweet or sour. Sweet cherries, such as 'Bing' and the decadently sweet 'Rainier' can be eaten right off the tree. Juicy and delicious, sweet cherries are best consumed without adornment. Their tart cousins, the sour cherry (also called tart cherries), include 'Nanking' and 'Montmorency' and are excellent choices for baking as long as a bit of sugar is added to sweeten them.

Cherry pies, crisps, and cobblers are mostly made using sour cherries, frequently also referred to as pie cherries. They are generally too tart to eat fresh from the tree.

Whether you grow sweet or sour cherries, plan to share a few with the wildlife in your area: birds love the fruits. Fortunately cherry trees are so prolific you can usually afford to share fruit with avian friends.

Cherry trees range in size from standard to semidwarf and dwarf. Space standard cherry trees 25 to 50 feet apart, semidwarfs 15 to 25 feet apart, and dwarfs 8 to 12 feet apart. If you plant an orchard of cherry trees (or just a few), choose small trees that are easy for harvesting.

With smooth-skinned fruit and a big pit, cherries are an exclusive fruit to the northern hemisphere. There are many cherry varieties, including wild species, that grow native in North America, Europe, and Asia. Sweet and sour cherries are cousins in the *Prunus* genus. The majority of sweet cherries are *Prunus avium*. The sour cherry is *Prunus cerasus*.

Sour cherries begin to bear 3 to 4 years after planting. Fruits ripen about 60 days after bloom, from late May to mid-June. Sweet cherries begin producing heavy yields in their fifth year and bear fruit in July. Store ripe cherries up to a week in the refrigerator.

Planting & Growing Tips

To plant a container-grown cherry tree, in a sunny location dig a hole the same depth as the length of the roots (about the depth of the container) and about twice as wide as the container. Firm the soil around the roots to eliminate air pockets in the soil.

Add protective netting to keep birds from eating cherries.

After you plant, clip off side branches of sweet cherries—but leave the leader.

recommended varieties

SOUR CHERRIES

'MONTMORENCY' is a medium to large sour cherry tree. It produces masses of large red fruit with yellow flesh. Zones 4 to 9.

'NORTHSTAR' is a heavy producer. Big harvests start in mid-June. 'Northstar' is hardy and disease-resistant. Zones 5 to 7.

'METEOR' is a 10-foot-tall sour cherry tree that bears bright red fruit with yellow flesh. It's a top choice for pie making and an ideal variety for home gardens. Zones 4 to 8.

'ENGLISH MORELLO' is late ripening with tart dark red to nearly black fruit. Zones 4 to 9.

SWEET CHERRIES

'BING' is the standard for sweet black cherries—and perfect for eating out of hand. The deep mahogany fruit is firm, juicy, and large. The large spreading tree yields large crops. Use 'Sam', 'Van', or 'Black Tartarian' as a pollenizer (not 'Royal Ann' or 'Lambert'). Zones 5 to 8.

'ROYAL ANN' is the standard for blushed yellow cherries. Trees bears large, firm, juicy fruit excellent for eating fresh or canning and preserves. The very large tree spreads with age. 'Royal Ann' is the cherry used to make maraschino cherries. Use 'Corum', 'Windsor', or 'Hedelfingen' as a pollenizer (not 'Bing' or 'Lambert'). Zones 5 to 8.

'RAINIER' features medium to large fruit with yellow skin that has a deep red blush. The sweet, firm, fine fruit has delicious yellow flesh. 'Ranier' ripens midseason. Zones 4 to 8.

'STELLA' is a sweet cherry with large, plump dark red fruit. The 25-foot-tall tree grows especially well in the South and West. 'Stella' is self-pollinating; you need only one tree. Zones 5 to 8.

Cherry 101

SITE: Cherries need a sunny location and fertile, well-drained soil. Bush type cherries can tolerate heavy and alkaline soils. Cherries thrive where winters and summers are mild.

BEDMATES: Sweet cherries require a pollinator. Plant two varieties. Sour or pie cherries are self-fertile—only one plant is necessary for fruit to set.

CARE: Prune sour cherry trees to form an open or vase shape. Prune sweet cherry trees to help form a central leader. After planting, clip off side branches but leave the leader.

HOW TO START: Purchase cherry trees as bare-root or container-grown plants.

HARVEST: Sour cherries begin to bear 3 to 4 years after planting. Fruits ripen about 60 days after flowers bloom. Harvest sour cherries from late May through mid-June. Sweet cherries produce heavy yields in their fifth year. Harvest fruits in July.

PESTS AND DISEASES: Cherry trees are susceptible to molds, including fusarium wilt, which becomes more prevalent in hot and humid conditions. Other common problems of cherry trees include plum curculio, brown rot, fruit flies, leaf spot, and bacterial canker.

Sweet Cherry Jam
Prep: 35 minutes   Process: 5 minutes

3	pounds fully ripe dark sweet cherries
1	1¾ ounce package regular powdered fruit pectin
1	teaspoon finely shredded lemon peel
¼	cup lemon juice
5	cups sugar

Sort, wash, stem, pit, and chop cherries. Measure 4 cups chopped cherries.

In a 6- or 8-quart Dutch oven or kettle combine cherries, pectin, lemon peel, and lemon juice. Bring to boiling on high heat, stirring constantly. Stir in sugar. Bring to a full rolling boil. Boil hard for 1 minute, stirring constantly. Remove from heat. Quickly skim off foam with a metal spoon.

Immediately ladle jam into hot, sterilized half-pint canning jars, leaving a ¼-inch headspace. Wipe jar rims and adjust lids. Process jars in a boiling-water canner for 5 minutes (start timing when water begins to boil). Remove jars from canner; cool on racks. Makes 6 half-pints (84 one-tablespoon servings).

Cherry Cobbler

Prep: 40 minutes   Bake: 20 minutes   Cool: 1 hour   Oven: 400°F

1	cup all-purpose flour
2	tablespoons sugar
1½	teaspoons baking powder
¼	teaspoon salt
½	teaspoon ground cinnamon (optional)
¼	cup butter or margarine
6	cups fresh or frozen unsweetened pitted tart red cherries
1	cup sugar
2	tablespoons cornstarch
1	egg
¼	cup milk
	Vanilla ice cream (optional)

Preheat oven to 400°F. For topping, in a medium bowl stir together flour, the 2 tablespoons sugar, the baking powder, salt, and, if desired, cinnamon. Cut in butter until mixture resembles coarse crumbs; set aside.

For filling, in a large saucepan combine the cherries, the 1 cup sugar, and the cornstarch. Cook on medium heat until cherries juice out, stirring occasionally. Continue to cook, stirring constantly, on medium heat until thickened and bubbly. Keep filling hot.

In a small bowl stir together egg and milk. Add to flour mixture, stirring just to moisten. Transfer hot filling to a 2-quart square baking dish. Using a spoon, immediately drop topping into 6 mounds on top of filling.

Bake for 20 to 25 minutes or until topping is golden brown. If desired, serve warm with ice cream. Makes 6 servings.

Blueberry Pie Filling (recipe on page 146)

Blueberries top most "best foods" lists because they are high in antioxidants. More good news is that they are delicious.

Flavorful Blueberries

Small, dark, sweet, and juicy,

the blueberry is fairly easy to grow and a treat to eat right off the bush. Blueberries are a favorite snack for kids—so small and easy to pop into small mouths—and a beautiful way to dress up a fresh green salad.

Cooked into jams, chutneys, or jellies, blueberries are keepers in more than one way: they make the most delicious preserves. Fans also love them sun-ripened and plucked right off the bush. Toss freshly washed berries onto a bowl of cereal or oatmeal, mix them into a fruit salad to add lovely dots and dashes of color, or simply sprinkle them on ice cream.

Blueberries are key players in recipes, where they add color and sweetness to muffins, turnovers, and pancakes. And pies! Blueberry pies are simply divine. So juicy and plump, blueberries are also extremely perishable. Store them unwashed in the refrigerator up to 1 week. To enjoy their fresh sweetness later in the season, rinse and dry berries and freeze them in single layers for long-term storage. The dark skins of blueberries deliver important health benefits, specifically antioxidants. In a recent study blueberries topped the list of fruit and vegetable competitors by rating highest in the capacity to destroy free radicals. Although you may think of blueberries as being a northern region fruit—the wild blueberry is the state fruit of Maine—southern states also grow this berry-producing shrub. There are blueberry varieties that are best suited for each region.

A true American native, the blueberry (*Vaccinium*) grows wild, although there are many domesticated forms. Blueberries are one of the few fruits native to North America. The most commonly raised blueberry is the highbush blueberry, which grows about 4 to 7 feet tall. Lowbush blueberries grow just 1 foot tall and spread by underground stems to form a dense mat. Blueberries can also be grown in containers.

Planting & Growing Tips

Tasty blue fruits and colorful red fall foliage make blueberries an outstanding addition to the landscape. Plant them in mixed shrub borders and perennial beds for structure and interest as well as fruit production.

Amend blueberry planting area soil by forking in ammonium sulfate.

Set bare-root stock at the same depth it was grown in the nursery, then cut back the plants by half to remove buds.

Dig holes 6 feet apart for highbush plants, 2 feet apart for lowbush, and 3 to 4 feet for dwarf or hedge highbush varieties.

Plant blueberries in the spring in northern zones and late fall in the South.

When soil isn't appropriate for blueberries (or space is limited), grow blueberries in containers. Choose big containers—at least 36 inches in diameter if you live in the North—and fill them with acidic potting mix. Water them so the soil stays moist but not wet.

Blueberries 101

SITE: Like most fruits, blueberries do best in full sun. They tolerate shade, but they won't produce nearly as much fruit as they would in full sun. They also prefer moist, well-drained soil that's rich in organic matter. If you have heavy clay, amend it with compost or peat moss before planting. Blueberries need soil with an acidic pH—ideally between 4.5 and 5.5. For neutral or alkaline soil, amend it with soil sulfur before planting blueberries.

BEDMATES: Most blueberries need another variety nearby to bear lots of fruit. Plant at least two varieties of the same type in your yard to ensure good harvests. Plant them in mixed shrub borders and perennial beds for structure and interest as well as fruit production.

CARE: In acidic soil, most blueberries are relatively low-maintenance once they become established. Remove all the flowers or fruits the year you plant them. After planting, spread a 3-inch-deep layer of mulch over the soil around the blueberries. Pull the mulch from the stems, leaving a gap of 1 or 2 inches to help prevent voles, mice, and other pests from attacking the blueberry from under the mulch. Water blueberries in times of drought, but don't let the soil stay soggy. If the soil tends to stay wet, plant blueberries in raised beds or containers to keep the roots from suffocating. For soil rich in organic matter, fertilizing your blueberries is not necessary—especially with mulch or top dressing with compost each season. Take caution if you fertilize because roots are very sensitive. Fertilize at one-half or one-quarter the recommended rate on the packaging.

HOW TO START: Buy blueberries in bare-root or container-grown forms.

HARVEST: Blueberries are ready to pick 2 to 4 months after flowering, from July to September. Ripening berries turn from green to pinkish red to blue, but not all blue ones are fully ripe.

PESTS AND DISEASES: Birds, deer, and raccoons feast on blueberries, so protect your crops, at least while they're young, with netting or fencing. Phomopsis canker, root rot, mummyberry, and twig blight can all affect blueberries. Japanese beetles are also a common blueberry pest.

recommended varieties

NORTHERN HIGHBUSH If you live in the Northeast, Midwest, Northwest, High Plains, or Mountain West, look for northern highbush blueberries. They have large fruits and are hardy in Zones 4 to 7. Common varieties include **'BLUECROP'**, **'EARLIBLUE'**, and **'JERSEY'**.

SOUTHERN HIGHBUSH If you live in the South or California, look for southern highbush varieties. They don't need as much winter cold to bear well, yet produce large, flavorful fruits. The plants are hardy in Zones 7 to 10. Popular varieties include **'ONEAL'**, **'OZARKBLUE'**, and **'LEGACY'**.

RABBITEYE Southern and Northwestern gardeners can grow rabbiteye blueberries, which are more compact shrubs than southern highbush types. The fruits tend to be smaller and appear later in the season. Rabbiteye varieties are hardy in Zones 7 to 9. Top rabbiteye varieties include **'PREMIER'** and **'POWDERBLUE'**.

LOWBUSH blueberry is a good choice for gardeners in the North. It has a groundcover habit and bears small, delicious fruits. It's hardy in Zones 3 to 6.

Blueberry Pie Filling

Prep: 30 minutes   Process: 30 minutes

8	quarts fresh blueberries
3	quarts water
8	cups sugar
3	cups ClearJel
9	cups cold water
⅓	cup bottled lemon juice

Rinse and drain blueberries. In a 6- to 8-quart kettle or pot heat the 3 quarts water to boiling. Add 8 cups of the blueberries; return to boiling. Using a slotted spoon, transfer berries to a very large bowl. Repeat with remaining berries, adding berries in 8-cup portions and returning water to boiling with each addition.

In a large saucepan combine sugar and ClearJel. Stir in the 9 cups cold water. Bring to boiling on medium-high heat, stirring constantly. Add lemon juice; boil for 1 minute, stirring constantly. Immediately pour over blueberries, stirring to coat.

Pack hot blueberry mixture into hot, sterilized quart canning jars, leaving a 1-inch headspace. Wipe jar rims; adjust lids. Process filled jars in a boiling-water canner for 30 minutes (start timing when water returns to boil). Remove jars from canner; cool on wire racks.

Spiced Blueberry Jam
Prep: 30 minutes   Process: 5 minutes

6   cups blueberries
2   tablespoons lemon juice
½   teaspoon ground cinnamon
¼   teaspoon ground allspice
      Dash ground cloves
7   cups sugar
1   6-ounce package (2 foil pouches) liquid
      fruit pectin

Crush blueberries with a potato masher. (You should have 4½ cups crushed berries.) In an 8- or 10-quart kettle or pot combine crushed blueberries, lemon juice, cinnamon, allspice, and cloves. Stir in sugar.

Heat on high heat to a full rolling boil, stirring constantly. Stir in pectin. Return to a full rolling boil. Boil hard for 1 minute, stirring constantly. Remove from heat; skim off foam with a metal spoon.

Ladle at once into hot, sterilized half-pint jars, leaving a ¼-inch headspace. Wipe jar rims; adjust lids. Process filled jars in a boiling-water canner for 5 minutes (start timing when water returns to boil). Remove jars from canner; cool on wire racks.

Chapter 5
Autumn

The growing season comes to fruition as the hot days of summer and nurturing spring rains fill out tree fruits, fatten tubers, and plump up pumpkins.

Fall Garden

As autumn's cooling temperatures signal a finale to the gardening season, extend crops by using inventive methods.

Season extending is a concept to use on both ends of the growing season. In early spring and late fall, cold threatens tender plants. Most annual plants will die when exposed to freezing temperatures. But with protection, vegetables will grow well past frost (and during early spring too). Here are a few ways to lengthen the growing season.

Cold Frame

A bottomless box with a skyward-facing window, a cold frame is a miniature greenhouse that extends the growing season by protecting plants and seeds from moderately cold temperatures and drying winds of late fall and early spring. Place one on a deck or patio to grow plants in pots or place one over a garden bed. Plan to grow cool-weather crops, such as radishes, spinach, and lettuce, and harvest to eat fresh well into winter.

Cloche

A cloche is bell-shape glass jar set over plants to protect them from extreme cold temperature. Place this portable structure over plants on nights when frost is expected.

Row Covers

Row covers are pieces of polyester fabric laid over plants. Covers help retain heat and protect plants from frost. Row covers are also effective in protecting plants from some pests and wind damage. Remove them during warm weather.

Milk Cartons

For an evening of frost protection, simple plastic milk cartons, with bottoms cut out, are frugal tools. Set them directly in the ground over plants that need protection.

Wall-O-Water

Like a mini greenhouse, a Wall-O-Water is a series of tubes filled with water that surrounds and protects individual plants.

FALL CLEANUP AND HARVEST

Fall is a productive time in the garden as some vegetables continue to be harvested.

POTATOES: After the foliage on potato plants has died back, use a fork to unearth these tubers.

ANNUALS: After frost most annuals fold like a house of cards. For examples, hot-weather crops such as tomatoes and peppers wither quickly. Pull withered plants and unripened fruits and add them to a compost bin.

COLD CROPS: Some vegetables, such as kale and Brussels sprouts, taste better after they've been exposed to cold weather. Leave these in the garden and continue to harvest after cold weather sets in.

TENDER PERENNIALS: Protect tender perennials, such as thyme and oregano, by adding a layer of mulch over the foliage to help insulate the plant roots from fluctuating temperatures and to conserve moisture.

COMBAT DISEASE: Use fall cleanup to combat diseases and pests. Remove and dispose of any diseased leaves. Don't compost foliage that has mold or other fungal diseases.

Pumpkin Crème Brûlée (recipe on page 156)

These orange orbs of autumn are so versatile—carve and cook them, and roast the seeds!

Surprising Pumpkins

Pumpkins are the most literary member of the squash family.

They appear in Washington Irving's "The Legend of Sleepy Hollow," the Brothers Grimm's "Cinderella," and the nursery rhyme "Peter, Peter, Pumpkin Eater." Add that to the fact that jack-'o-lanterns are the most recognizable Halloween icon, and you can be sure that every kid knows what a pumpkin is. That's why growing pumpkins (*Cucurbita*) with kids is so fun. Plus there are so many mini varieties to choose from such as 'Jack-Be-Little' and white-skinned 'Baby Boo'. Planting pumpkins is a surefire way to get your kids excited about gardening.

Pumpkins are synonymous with Halloween decor as well as the main pie ingredient at Thanksgiving, although most pumpkin fans have never actually eaten fresh pumpkin. And that's a shame—because fresh pumpkin is sweet, delicious, plentiful, and inexpensive in autumn. If you have a big patch of open flat land, you can grow your own pumpkins to use as autumn decor and in pumpkin recipes that range from soup to nuts (literally, because you can eat the seeds roasted to crisp, nutty perfection).

To raise pumpkins for eating, grow specific varieties for this purpose. Sweet, firm flesh can be baked, boiled, and sauteed. As in most deep-hued vegetables, pumpkins are rich in beta-carotene, an antioxidant.

Planting & Growing Tips

Start pumpkins early in the season indoors, but don't plant pumpkin seeds (or seedlings) until well after frost is past.

Form a mound of soil about 8 to 10 inches high and plant several seeds 1 inch deep in the top of the mound. Remove smaller seedlings when sprouts have 2 or 3 leaves. The ideal pumpkin hill should have 2 to 3 large plants per hill.

Separate hills 4 to 8 feet apart.

Water plants if rainfall is scarce, although pumpkins tolerate short periods of hot, dry weather. Create a slow-drip irrigation system by making a hole in an aluminum can and burying it next to the plant. Fill with water in drought situations.

Create a "pumpkin coaster"—a barrier between the fruit and the ground so the pumpkin doesn't rot. Use mulch or straw.

Pumpkins 101

SITE: Choose a large, sunny spot so pumpkin plants can spread out. Pumpkins do best in slightly acid soil. Soil should also drain easily. Amend with well-composted manure.

BEDMATES: Pumpkins can share space with corn, melons, and other squash. However, pumpkins are space hogs and need a lot of room on their own.

CARE: Keep pumpkin vines free of weeds by shallow hoeing around plants.

HOW TO START: Sow seeds directly in the ground when the soil/air temperatures reach at least 70°F. Start seeds ahead of the season and plant seedlings too.

HARVEST: Generally, begin harvest in late September or early October—before a hard frost. Pick pumpkins when they are a deep, solid color (depending on variety, this may be orange, white, or cream). Wear gloves (vines have prickles on the stems) and use a pair of pruning shears or a sharp knife to cut each pumpkin from its vine. Leave 3 to 4 inches of stem attached (pumpkins with stems keep longer than those without). If pumpkin vines look sickly or die early, pick pumpkins and store them in a dry place.

PESTS AND DISEASES: Pumpkins are susceptible to fungal diseases such as powdery mildew. Look for a white powder on the tops of the leaves. Treat with a fungicide. Insects attracted to pumpkins include cucumber beetles and squash bugs; they will attack seedlings, vines, and developing fruit. Watch for these pests especially in late summer. If you use insecticides, apply in late afternoon or early evening after pumpkin blossoms have closed so bees are not adversely affected.

recommended varieties

'LONG ISLAND CHEESE' is a slightly flat, buff-orange pumpkin that resembles a wheel of cheese. The flesh is mild and sweet and excellent for pies. Fruits grow 6 to 10 pounds. Try 'Autumn Crown' for a mini version.

'SMALL SUGAR' is the standard pumpkin-pie squash. It measures about 10 inches in diameter. The skin is orange-yellow and the flesh is sweet and fine-grained. It keeps well too.

'BABY PAM' gets lots of votes for the best pie pumpkin. The 4-pound pumpkins have beautiful deep orange skins. The flesh is sweet and dry; 4 to 5 pumpkins per plant.

'BABY BEAR' is a 1- to 2-pound deep orange pumpkin with a flat shape. Kids love harvesting this pumpkin because it's just the right size. It produces semihulless seeds that are ideal for roasting.

Pumpkin Crème Brûlée

Prep: 35 minutes   Roast: 20 minutes   Bake: 70 minutes
Cool: 80 minutes   Chill: 2 hours   Oven: 350°F

6	small (about 1½ pounds each) sugar pumpkins
15	egg yolks
4	cups whipping cream
1¼	cups granulated sugar
¼	cup cooked pumpkin puree
1	tablespoon vanilla
	Sugared Pumpkin Seeds

Preheat oven to 350°F. Cut tops off each pumpkin and , if desired, reserve for presentations. Scrape out the seeds and fibers from pumpkins (reserve seeds for Sugared Pumpkin Seeds). Place pumpkins on a baking sheet, cut sides up, and roast, uncovered, for 20 minutes. Remove from oven and cool for 20 minutes.

In a large mixing bowl combine egg yolks, cream, sugar, pumpkin puree, and vanilla. Beat with a whisk just until combined. Divide the mixture evenly among the 6 cooled pumpkins.

Place the pumpkins in a large roasting pan and set on the oven rack. Pour hot water into the pan to reach halfway up the pumpkins. Bake for 70 to 80 minutes or until a knife inserted near the center of the crème brûlées comes out clean. (If using, place reserved pumpkin tops on a baking sheet the last 25 minutes of baking; cool and chill until serving time.) Remove pumpkins from pan and cool on a wire rack for 1 hour. Cover and chill for 2 to 24 hours.

To serve, sprinkle with Sugared Pumpkin Seeds. Set reserved pumpkin tops on the plates, if using. Makes 6 large servings.

SUGARED PUMPKIN SEEDS: Preheat oven to 325°F. Line a shallow baking pan with foil; grease the foil. Set pan aside. Rinse pumpkin seeds to remove strings and pulp. Drain well. Place about ²/₃ cup seeds in prepared pan. Bake, uncovered, for 1 hour. Drizzle with 1 tablespoon melted butter and sprinkle with 2 teaspoons

Roasted Pumpkin Seeds
Prep: 15 minutes   Stand: 24 hours   Bake: 40 minutes   Oven: 325°F

- 4¼ **cups raw pumpkin seeds**
- 2 **tablespoons cooking oil**
- 1 **teaspoon salt**

Rinse pumpkin seeds in water until pulp and strings are washed off, then drain.

In a medium bowl combine pumpkin seeds, cooking oil, and salt. Spread mixture onto a waxed paper-lined 15×10×1-inch baking pan. Let stand for 24 to 48 hours or until dry, stirring occasionally.

Preheat oven to 325°F. Remove waxed paper from baking pan. Toast seeds for 40 minutes, stirring once or twice. Spread seeds on paper towels. Makes 16 (¼-cup) servings.

Creamy Apple Pie

Prep: 1 hour   Bake: 10 minutes   Cool: 15 minutes
Chill: 4 hours   Oven: 350°F

Nonstick cooking spray
2 **cups crushed crunchy oat and honey granola bars (about 12 bars)**
1 **cup flaked coconut**
¼ **cup butter, melted**
2 **tablespoons butter**
½ **cup packed brown sugar**
1 **tablespoon lemon juice**
1 **teaspoon ground cinnamon**
7 **large cooking apples, peeled, cored, and thickly sliced (about 3½ pounds)**
1 **8-ounce carton mascarpone cheese or one 8-ounce package cream cheese, softened**
¼ **cup granulated sugar**
2 **tablespoons amaretto or ½ teaspoon almond extract**
1 **cup whipping cream**

Preheat oven to 350°F. Coat a 9-inch pie plate with cooking spray.

Combine crushed bars, coconut, and ¼ cup butter. Press on bottom and up sides of pie plate. Bake 10 minutes. Cool. In very large skillet melt 2 tablespoons butter on medium heat. Stir in brown sugar, lemon juice, and cinnamon. Stir in apples. Cook, uncovered, on medium heat for 25 minutes or until apples are very tender, stirring occasionally.

Cool 15 minutes. Meanwhile, in a large bowl beat cheese, granulated sugar, and amaretto on medium for 30 seconds or until light and fluffy. In a medium mixing bowl beat whipping cream on medium until soft peaks form; beat into mascarpone mixture on low until combined. Layer half the apple mixture in piecrust. Spread half the cheese-whipped cream mixture on the apples. Layer remaining apple mixture on cheese-whipped cream mixture. Spread with remaining cheese-whipped cream mixture. Cover loosely and refrigerate at least 4 hours or up to 24 hours. Makes 8 to 10 servings.

Get out the bushel baskets for big harvests of red, yellow, and green apples.

Tart & Sweet Apples

The old adage "An apple a day keeps the doctor away"

is based on the health benefits of this fruit. This self-packaged, easy-to-carry fruit has no fat, no sodium, and no cholesterol. At about 80 calories a serving, apples are an ample source of antioxidants and fiber (each apple delivers 5 grams of fiber). To get that fiber boost, eat apples with skins on. Two-thirds of the fiber is in the peel.

If you love the crisp taste of a fresh apple,

you should plant a tree or two in your yard. Apple trees (*Malus*) have three sizes: dwarf, semi-dwarf, and standard. Because apple tree varieties are generally grafted onto different rootstocks, you can usually pick the apple you want in one of these three sizes. The smallest apple trees are dwarfs that grow to about 10 feet tall. Semi-dwarfs reach about 15 feet. And standard-size apple trees grow to 20 feet or more.

For most small yards, dwarf and semi-dwarf apple trees are space-conscious choices. Their small size allows for planting more than one. Even though these trees are small in stature, they still produce a lot of fruit. Once a dwarf apple tree starts bearing, it provides 3 to 6 bushels of fruit. A semi-dwarf tree can produce 6 to 10 bushels of apples. With one bushel weighing 42 pounds, at the minimum you'll get more than 100 pounds of apples from a dwarf tree.

In addition to prolific fruit production, another reason to raise your own apples is to grow heirlooms and rare varieties not available in stores—or even local farmers' markets. Add apple trees to your landscape plan—a well-pruned tree offers flowers in the spring, apples during the summer and fall, and interesting shape during winter (once the leaves fall).

For small spaces, grow trees in pots or train them to grow horizontally (a method called espalier). Columnar varieties are space-conscious and produce ample fruit. You may have to wait 3 to 5 years after planting for the first full harvest, but sweet, homegrown apples are worth the wait.

Planting & Growing Tips

Plant apple trees in late spring after the soil is thawed. Dig a hole 2 feet wider than the spread of the tree roots; plant the tree at the same depth as it was in the nursery pot. Keep the graft union 2 inches above the soil line.

Train young trees to a modified central leader and thin the branches to 1 to 2 inches apart. To train apples against a wall or building—espalier—start with a young tree.

Prune each year during the dormant season. Work at creating wide crotch angles, which are stronger and less prone to breaking.

Grow apple trees in containers. Try dwarf and columnar varieties.

Thinning fruit (removing apples growing really close together) results in larger mature fruit.

Apples 101

SITE: Apples require full sun and well-drained soil. Site apple trees in areas that receive at least 6 hours of sun a day.

BEDMATES: Plant multiple apple trees for cross-pollination. Apples bear best when there are two varieties nearby to pollinate each other. Some apples have to be pollinated by another variety to bear fruit. Be sure to note special needs such as this when you select varieties for your yard.

CARE: Pruning apple trees yearly helps them keep their shape and encourages fruit production. Start pruning while trees are young. Help encourage a central leader. In the late winter prune apple trees to thin branches to 1 to 2 feet apart. Once trees set fruit, thin fruit on full-size apple trees by hand: one apple per spur. Fertilize apple trees with a general-purpose timed-release plant food each spring to ensure the tree has enough nutrients to bear a healthy crop of apples.

APPLES IN CONTAINERS: If you have large containers (at least 4 to 5 feet in diameter), you can grow apples in pots. Choose dwarf varieties, which won't become too large for the containers. Fill the pots with a high-quality potting mix. It's best not to use garden soil as it doesn't drain well in containers. In Zone 6 and warmer, you can leave the pots outdoors all year. In colder climates, it's best to move the trees to a protected spot, such as an unheated garage or storage shed, for the winter. Keep container-grown apple trees well watered.

HOW TO START: Buy bare-root or container-grown apple trees. Although you can start apple trees from seed, it takes a long time before these plants bear fruit.

HARVEST: There are early-, mid-, and late-maturing apple varieties, so the harvest season can stretch from August to October. Apples ripen in 70 to 180 days from bloom, depending on the variety. Pick apples from the tree when they separate easily from the branch and have firm flesh. Soft apples are overripe but can be used for cooking. Store them in a cool spot (under 40°F) after harvest.

PESTS AND DISEASES: There are middle- and late-season apples. Early-season apples are the most susceptible to apple maggot. Spray infestations with insecticidal soap. Use dormant oil spray in the late winter (before the buds start to swell) to control codling moths, plum curculios, scale, leaf rollers, mites, and aphids.

recommended varieties

EARLY FALL HARVEST

'ANNA' produces green apples with red blush. This early-season apple is suited for Florida and Southern California. Pair it with early-flowering varieties to ensure pollination. Zones 5 to 9.

'ROYAL GALA' was introduced to North America from New Zealand. This crisp, juicy apple has red striping on its yellow-tinged skin. An early producer, it ripens in August. A great fresh apple, it is also good for pies, crisps, and applesauce. Zones 3 to 8.

'GINGER GOLD' is an early-ripening apple. Sweet, firm, and delicious, 'Ginger Gold' doesn't keep long, so enjoy while you have them. Zones 5 to 9.

'LODI' is a green-skinned apple and one of the earliest to produce. It's also among the best of the cooking apples. Zones 4 to 8.

MID-FALL HARVEST

'JONATHAN' bears small to medium crisp, dark red apples with yellowish white flesh and a tart flavor. A good all-purpose apple. Zones 5 to 9.

'GOLDEN DELICIOUS' produces firm, crisp, round apples. The flesh is sweet and juicy—a good all-purpose apple for pies, crisps, applesauce, or eating fresh. Zones 4 to 7.

'RED DELICIOUS' apples have five bumps on the blossom end of each fruit, making them easy to identify. Sweet, juicy apples taste great from the tree but are not recommended for baking. Zones 5 to 9.

'McINTOSH' bears medium to large bright red apples with sweet, juicy white flesh. A good all-purpose apple. Zones 3 to 9.

'HONEYCRISP' produces medium fruit with mottled red and yellow skin. It has a crisp, juicy texture and a sweet flavor highlighted with a touch of tartness. 'Honeycrisp' is an excellent storage apple. Zones 3 to 9.

'CORTLAND' features red apples with a white center. Perfect for pies, crisps, and cider. Zones 4 to 6.

'LADY' is an heirloom variety with excellent storage ability. The small to medium fruit has green skin with red blush and ripens late in the season. Zones 5 to 8.

'JONAGOLD', a blend of 'Jonathan' and 'Golden Delicious', offers tangy sweetness. A great choice for eating straight off the tree as well as for baked or cooked apple recipes. Zones 5 to 9.

'GRANNY SMITH' has glossy, bright green fruit that is medium to large in size. It has a very tart flavor and is good for fresh eating and cooking. The tree is strong and vigorous but requires a very long growing season. Zones 6 to 8.

Cheddar-Apple Bundles
Prep: 45 minutes   Bake: 20 minutes   Cool: 20 minutes   Oven: 400°F

½   cup packed brown sugar
½   cup chopped pecans
2   cups all-purpose flour
8   ounce white cheddar cheese, shredded
    (2 cups)
1   tablespoon granulated sugar
½   cup butter, cut up
6   to 8 tablespoons cold water
2   medium Granny Smith or Jonathan apples,
    peeled, cored, and chopped (about 2 cups)
3   tablespoons fig jam or apricot preserves

Combine brown sugar and pecans; set aside. In a food processor combine flour, ½ cup of the cheese, granulated sugar, and ¼ teaspoon salt; cover and process with one on/off turn. Add butter. Cover; process with several on/off turns until size of small peas. With processor running, slowly add water to make dough come together in a ball. Gently knead until smooth.

Preheat oven to 400°F. Divide dough in 8 pieces. For each bundle, on floured surface roll dough to 8-inch circles. Place 3 tablespoons cheese and ¼ cup apple in center. Sprinkle with 1 tablespoon nut mixture. Brush dough edges with water. Bring up dough edges and press together to seal. Place on parchment-lined baking sheet, sealed sides up. Bake 20 to 25 minutes or until pastry is golden. Spoon preserves on each bundle. Cool 20 minutes on baking sheet. Serve warm. Makes 8 servings.

Praline Baked Apple

Prep: 15 minutes   Bake: 30 minutes
Oven: 350°F

¼   **cup apple juice or apple cider**
    Dash ground cinnamon
2   **small red baking apples**
2   **tablespoons pecans or walnuts,
    coarsely chopped**
2   **tablespoons brown sugar**
    Dash ground cinnamon
    **Vanilla low-fat frozen yogurt or ice
    cream (optional)**

Preheat oven to 350°F.

In a small bowl combine apple juice and dash cinnamon. Divide the mixture between two 6-ounce custard cups. Core apples; remove peel from the top of each apple. Place the apples in the custard cups.

Place the custard cups in a shallow baking pan. In another small bowl combine pecans, brown sugar, and cinnamon. Sprinkle over the apples.

Bake, covered, for 30 to 40 minutes or until apples are tender. If desired, serve the baked apples with frozen yogurt.

harvest tip

Pick apples by hand to avoid bruising them. A ripe apple separates easily from the branch and has firm flesh.

Herbed Grilled Potatoes
Prep: 25 minutes Grill: 16 minutes

2	pounds small red, yellow, and/or purple potatoes, halved
2	tablespoons olive oil
½	teaspoon salt
½	teaspoon freshly ground black pepper
1	to 2 tablespoons chopped fresh parsley, basil, and/or rosemary

In a large covered saucepan cook potatoes in enough boiling salted water to cover for 6 to 8 minutes or just until potatoes are tender. Drain.

In a large bowl gently toss potatoes with 1 tablespoon of the oil, the salt, and pepper. Transfer potatoes to a grill pan.

Place grill pan on a grill rack directly over medium heat. Grill for 16 to 18 minutes or until potatoes are tender and brown, stirring occasionally.

To serve, transfer potatoes to a serving bowl. Toss with remaining olive oil and fresh herbs. Serve warm. Makes 8 appetizer or 4 side-dish servings.

With so many varieties to choose from, you'll find yourself looking for more garden space.

Colorful Potatoes

So easy to grow and so delicious.

You'll want to have hills of potatoes in your garden. *Solanum tuberosum* is an annual vegetable crop planted in early spring and harvested in autumn. It takes 2 to 4 months for the crop to mature. Harvest "new" potatoes in as little as 6 weeks. These subterranean tubers are grown from seed potatoes, which are pieces of mature potatoes. With more than 4,000 types of potatoes to choose from, you won't have any trouble finding one or several to grow.

Potatoes, originally from Peru, are part of nearly every culture's cuisine. From the classic American teenager food of choice, the french fry, to Ireland's colcannon, Italy's gnocchi, and Quebec's poutine, the humble potato plays a large role in the world's favorite comfort-food dishes.

Potato varieties offer a rainbow of colors (skin and flesh can be different hues). Potatoes can have skins that are red, white, yellow, or purple. Flesh color can range from blue to yellow and snow white. Potatoes also have a wide variety of sizes, from small fingerlings to giant spuds that weigh several pounds each. Flesh consistency is different too and that influences how to cook them. For example, floury potatoes are used for baking and have more starch than waxy potatoes, which are better for boiling.

The earthy taste of freshly dug potatoes is sublime. Plucked from your backyard garden, these tender, juicy gems can be prepared so many ways: boiled, roasted, fried, and mashed. A medium-size potato prepared with skin on provides 27 mg of vitamin C (45 percent of the daily requirement). Potatoes are high in fiber (2 grams per average serving).

harvest tip
When the tops of the potato plants start to die back, it's time to dig up these luscious tubers.

Planting & Growing Tips

Plant seed potatoes, cutting up whole potatoes into pieces that have "eyes." Allow the pieces to dry overnight before planting. Place cut potatoes in a 4- to 6-inch trench with the eyes up. Space rows 12 to 15 inches apart.

Hill or mound the soil around the base of the stems as the potato plants get larger. This give more underground space for the potatoes to grow.

Harvest new potatoes by digging down beside the stem and removing individual tubers. Harvest new (or young small) potatoes 6 to 8 weeks after planting.

Dig mature potatoes with a fork, taking care not to spear them as you unearth them.

Potatoes 101

SITE: Potatoes need a sunny location with well-drained soil.

BEDMATES: Rotate growing beds. Don't plant potatoes in garden space where tomatoes or eggplant were grown the previous season. Tomatoes, eggplant, and potatoes are in the same family and may attract similar pests and diseases.

CARE: Keep the soil in the potato bed consistently moist but not wet. Potatoes require fertilizer higher in phosphorus and potassium than nitrogen. Once the tubers sprout, begin mounding (hilling) the soil around the bottom of the stems when the plants reach about 6 inches tall. Continue to mound the soil as the plants grow taller. Hilling creates the soil area where potato tubers develop—plus it keeps tubers from being exposed to the sun. Cover any potatoes that are exposed or poking out of the soil; otherwise they will turn green and become inedible because they develop a mild toxin.

HOW TO START: Plant potatoes from seed potatoes or pieces of sprouting tubers.

HARVEST: Early potato varieties can be dug as new potatoes as soon as they are large enough—about 6 to 8 weeks after planting when tubers are 1 to 2 inches in diameter. Serve them with spring peas or fresh greens—also ready for harvest in early spring. Harvest new potatoes by digging next to the stems with a small garden fork. To grow larger potatoes, wait until the plant tops start to die back on their own, then harvest. Store potatoes in a dark, humid location at 65°F to 70°F for 2 weeks. For long-term storage, place tubers in the dark at 40°F to 50°F.

PESTS AND DISEASES: Potatoes have a variety of diseases. Avoid many of them by selecting virus-resistant varieties. Scab can be prevented by keeping soil pH acidic. Use a fungicide to prevent anthracnose. A variety of insects find potatoes appealing. Pick off and destroy beetles, worms, and caterpillars. Colorado potato beetles can be controlled by shaking them off plants and destroying them. Use Bt or neem if insect infestations get out of hand. Use insecticidal soap to control leafhoppers. If there are flea beetles in your area, use floating row covers to protect young plants.

recommended varieties:
best spuds for the taste buds

There are hundreds of potato varieties in all colors of the rainbow. Here's a selection of some of the prettiest and tastiest.

'ALL BLUE' Blue outside and in, this medium-size potato really gives a meal color. Try it steamed, sauteed, or sliced and diced in a gratin dish.

'CRANBERRY RED' Also known as 'All Red', this large potato features a smooth, moist texture and is an excellent candidate for steaming and sautéing. It's a star in gratin dishes as well.

'ELBA' The albino of potatoes, this large white-skin, white-flesh variety is tops for baking or boiling. It's also a treat in salads because it holds its shape well when cooked.

'ISLAND SUNSHINE' With golden-white skin and golden flesh, this medium-size round potato tastes good baked, fried, or boiled.

'ONAWAY' A round white potato, this variety is a reliable grower and ripens early. Its moist texture and shape hold up when boiled. Try it in soups, stews, and salads.

'REDDALE' Blushing red on the outside and white inside, this large potato has moist flesh that's well suited for boiling, salads, soups, and stews.

'ROSE GOLD' As its name suggests, this medium potato boasts rosy red skin and golden flesh. Its high straight-starch content makes it perfect baked, steamed, or in cream soups.

'RUSSIAN BANANA' This golden-skin fingerling potato has crescent-shape tapered ends and is an heirloom variety that was grown by Russian settlers. It's especially tasty baked, boiled, and in salads.

'SWEDISH PEANUT' A dry, golden-flesh heirloom variety from Sweden, also known as 'Mandel', this fingerling potato makes the taste buds sing when it's roasted or mashed.

'YUKON GOLD' This golden-flesh potato is an especially good keeper and an all-around winner. Wood Prairie Farm's best seller, it's ideal for baking, frying, and boiling.

All Blue

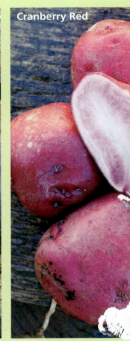

Cranberry Red

Reddale

Rose Gold

Elba

Island Sunshine

Onaway

Russian Banana

Swedish Peanut

Yukon Gold

Walnut-Sage Potatoes au Gratin

Prep: 30 minutes Bake: 70 minutes
Stand: 10 minutes Oven: 350°F

6	medium Yukon gold or Finnish yellow potatoes (2 pounds)
½	cup chopped onion
2	cloves garlic, minced
3	tablespoons walnut oil
3	tablespoons all-purpose flour
½	teaspoon salt
¼	teaspoon freshly ground black pepper
2½	cups milk
3	tablespoons snipped fresh sage
1	cup shredded Gruyère cheese (4 ounces)
⅓	cup broken walnut pieces
	Fresh sage leaves (optional)

Preheat oven to 350°F. Peel potatoes, if desired, and thinly slice (should have 6 cups). Place slices in a colander. Rinse with cool water; drain.

For sauce: In a medium saucepan on medium heat, cook onion and garlic in walnut oil until tender but not brown. Stir in flour, salt, and pepper. Add milk all at once. Cook and stir on medium heat until thickened and bubbly. Remove from heat; stir in the snipped sage.

Grease a 2- to 2½-quart rectangular baking dish or 2-quart round glass casserole. Layer half the potatoes in dish. Cover with half the sauce. Sprinkle with half the cheese. Repeat layering with the potatoes and sauce. (Cover and chill the remaining Gruyère cheese until needed.)

Bake, covered, for 40 minutes. Uncover; bake 25 minutes more or until potatoes are tender. Sprinkle remaining cheese and the walnuts on top. Bake, uncovered, for 5 minutes more. Let stand 10 minutes before serving. If desired, garnish with sage leaves. Makes 10 to 12 servings.

Sicilian Potato Croquettes

Prep: 30 minutes Cook: 3 minutes/batch
Oven: 200°F

2	pounds boiling potatoes, such as Russet or Yukon gold, peeled and quartered
1¾	teaspoons salt
2	egg yolks
⅓	cup grated Romano cheese
¼	cup chopped green onions
¼	cup pine nuts
3	tablespoons snipped fresh parsley
3	tablespoons snipped fresh mint
¼	teaspoon freshly ground black pepper
	Cooking oil for deep-fat frying
3	egg whites
½	cup all-purpose flour
1	cup plain fine dry bread crumbs

In a large covered saucepan cook potatoes and 1 teaspoon of the salt in enough cold water to cover by 2 inches for 12 to 15 minutes or until tender. Drain. Press potatoes through a potato ricer or food mill into a large bowl. Beat in the remaining ¾ teaspoon salt, egg yolks, Romano cheese, green onions, pine nuts, parsley, mint, and pepper.

Heat oven to 200°F. Line 2 shallow baking pans with foil. For each croquette, shape a rounded tablespoon of the potato mixture in a 2-inch oval. Place ovals in prepared pans.

In a large heavy saucepan or very large deep skillet heat oil to 365°F on medium heat. Beat egg whites until frothy. Spread flour in a shallow dish and bread crumbs in another shallow dish. Dip potato croquettes in flour, then egg whites, then coat in crumbs.

Fry croquettes, 5 or 6 at a time, in hot oil until golden, about 3 minutes. Remove croquettes with a slotted spoon and drain on paper towels. Keep croquettes warm in the oven while frying the remaining ovals. Serve warm. Makes 30 croquettes.

Pear-Pecan Stuffing

Prep: 30 minutes   Bake: 40 minutes   Oven 350°F

1	pound firm-texture white sandwich bread
2	tablespoons butter (no substitutes)
1	large onion, chopped (1 cup)
2	large firm ripe Bartlett pears, cored, peeled, and chopped
½	to ¾ cup water
¼	cup butter (no substitutes)
1	cup pecan halves, toasted and coarsely chopped
2	tablespoons snipped fresh Italian (flat-leaf) parsley
¼	teaspoon freshly grated nutmeg
⅛	teaspoon salt
	Dash freshly ground black pepper

Preheat oven to 350°F.

Spread bread slices on baking sheets. Place baking sheets in the oven for 20 minutes or until bread is dry.

Place the 2 tablespoons butter, the onion, and pears in a large skillet; cook on medium heat until tender but not brown, about 4 minutes. Set aside.

Break the dried bread into small pieces. Place in a very large bowl. Bring ½ cup water and the ¼ cup butter to boiling in a small saucepan. Add to bread crumbs; toss just until moistened.

Stir in pear mixture, pecans, parsley, nutmeg, salt, and pepper. Add the remaining water until mixture reaches desired moistness. Stuff turkey and roast in a 325°F oven or transfer stuffing to a 2-quart casserole and bake, covered, in a 325°F or 350°F oven about 40 minutes or until heated through. Makes 12 to 14 servings.

Easy to grow
and attractive
in any landscape,
pear trees
are impressive
fruit producers.

Plump Pears

This fruit has a long, glamorous history, reaping rave

reviews even in ancient times. Homer refers to the pear as a gift of the gods in *The Odyssey*. Succulent and shapely, the pear was also revered for its long storage life, an important trading commodity in the ancient world. Loved as a fruit, it was also appreciated for its painterly form—pears have long been popular still-life subjects for European painters.

Pears are not native to North America, but they were among the many crops early colonists brought for food for their settlements. A popular kitchen garden fruit tree, pears (*Pyrus*) offer a range of fruit options. Choose from many delicious varieties for home gardens such as the popular sweet, green 'Bartlett'; the shapely, sweet and juicy 'Bosc'; and the tiny 'Seckel' dessert pear.

Pear trees can be trained into a formal or informal appearance—and they are one of the easiest of the fruit trees to grow. For small landscapes or a kitchen garden, choose the smallest pear, a dwarf. If you have space for one tree, select a self-pollinating (or self-fruitful) type. Otherwise pears need a pollinator, and more than one is needed.

Pear trees bloom in spring and produce small white buds that unfurl into single-petal white flowers. If there is a late frost while the tree is in flower, it's a bitter disappointment for pear lovers because frost often means there is no fruit for the year.

For fresh fruit or to can the bounty, a pear will not disappoint. These big producers bear bushels of succulent fruit. A fresh, juicy pear is wonderful; cooking with pears is equally delicious. Firm varieties, such as 'Bosc' or 'Anjou', are best choices for poaching, baking, and grilling. Their dense flesh holds their shape. Soft pears, such as 'Yellow Bartlett', 'Red Bartlett', and 'Comice' are not good candidates for cooking because they become squishy and their flavor diminishes. Eat these lovelies fresh.

Planting & Growing Tips

To plant a bare-root or container-grown pear, dig a hole large enough to allow the roots to spread out completely. Backfill the planting hole with topsoil.

Dwarf pear trees have graft unions (where the variety was grafted onto rootstock); make sure when planting that these are 2 to 3 inches above the soil surface.

Pears don't need to be pruned as much as other fruit trees. However, you should prune standard trees to a central leader. In late winter or early spring head back side branches so they don't compete with the central leader.

After normal fruit drop, thin the remaining fruits for best size.

Grow dwarf varieties as hedges or prune them into espalier forms.

Pears 101

SITE: Choose a sunny, well-drained location. Pears are deep rooted and can grow in any soil but do best in rich, heavy loam.

BEDMATES: If you plant one pear, choose a self-pollinating type. Otherwise, pears need a cross pollinator—two or more varieties.

CARE: No need to fertilize a newly planted pear tree. Wait to feed until after the soil around the roots is thoroughly settled (2 to 3 weeks after planting).

HOW TO START: Plant bare-root or container-grown trees.

HARVEST: Pear trees bear based on size: standard trees produce fruit in 5 to 6 years; dwarf trees bear fruit faster—in just 3 to 4 years. Pick pears in August through September. Pick pears 1 to 2 weeks before they are completely ripe. Pears should ripen at room temperature. To store fresh pears, keep them in a cool, dark place, then bring them out to ripen for eating.

PESTS AND DISEASES: Pear trees are susceptible to fire blight. Prune off affected branches and destroy. Fire blight is a bacterial disease with no cure. Another disease, pear psylla, can be controlled by spraying with dormant oil spray in late winter or early spring. To control pear scab and pests, rake up and remove windfall fruits and leaves. Protect tree trunks from bark-eating rabbits or mice by wrapping hardware cloth or plastic guards around the lower portion of trunks.

recommended varieties

'BARTLETT' is a popular pear with large yellow fruit and smooth, juicy white flesh. Zones 5 to 7.

'BOSC' has a unique sweet-spice flavor and brown skin. These firm fruits have a long neck and a full rounded base. Zones 5 to 8.

'HOSUI ASIAN' is a round pear with a snappy tang for taste. The blight-resistant tree is self-pollinating. Zones 5 to 9.

'KIEFFER' is an oval Oriental pear with yellow-green skin splashed with red when ripe. The white flesh is crisp and juicy with coarse texture. Zones 4 to 9.

'SECKEL' produces small fruit early in the season with intense sweet flavor. They store well and the trees are resistant to fire blight. Zones 4 to 8.

'SHINKO ASIAN' bears medium to large fruit with golden-brown skin and creamy flesh. The fruit is sweet and juicy, and the tree is an excellent producer. Zones 4 to 9.

Pear-Blue Cheese Salad

Start to Finish: 25 minutes

2	tablespoons butter
1	cup pecan halves
1	tablespoon sugar
⅛	teaspoon salt
16	cups torn curly endive (chicory), romaine lettuce, or spinach
3	ripe pears, cored and thinly sliced
1	cup crumbled blue cheese
¾	cup purchased vinaigrette

In a large skillet melt butter on medium heat. Add pecan halves. Cook 4 to 5 minutes or until pecans are lightly toasted, stirring frequently. Sprinkle sugar and salt over pecans; cook and stir for 1 minute more. Transfer pecans to a medium bowl; cool.

In a 6- to 8-quart salad bowl combine curly endive, pears, blue cheese, and half the pecans. Pour vinaigrette over salad. Toss gently to coat. Divide among salad plates. Sprinkle with remaining pecans. Makes 8 servings.

TEST KITCHEN TIP: To serve on a buffet, add only about ¼ cup dressing; serve remaining dressing on the side.

harvest tip

Harvest pears when they have reached full size but are still green and firm. To pick, lift the pear with a twisting motion rather than pulling on it.

Fresh Pear and Cranberry Pie

Prep: 35 minutes   Bake: 70 minutes
Cool: 1½ hours   Oven: 375°F

- **1   recipe Pastry for a Single-Crust Pie**
- **8   cups sliced red and/or green ripe pears (7 to 8 pears; 3 to 3½ pounds total)**
- **1   cup fresh cranberries**
- **¼   cup sugar**
- **3   tablespoons cornstarch**
- **2   tablespoons apple cider or water**
- **¼   teaspoon ground nutmeg**
- **1   tablespoon sugar**
- **2   tablespoons caramel-flavor ice cream topping, plus additional for drizzling**

Prepare and roll out Pastry for Single-Crust Pie. Preheat oven to 375°F.

Arrange half the pears in prepared pastry; sprinkle with half the cranberries. Arrange remaining pears on cranberries. In a bowl stir together ¼ cup sugar, cornstarch, cider, and nutmeg; drizzle evenly over pears. Cover pie with foil.

Bake 40 minutes. Remove foil; sprinkle with 1 tablespoon sugar. Bake, uncovered, 30 to 35 minutes more or until pears are tender and juices are bubbly. Remove from oven and place on wire rack.

Meanwhile, in a small saucepan combine remaining cranberries and 2 tablespoons caramel topping. Bring to boiling. Cook 1 minute. Remove from heat. Spoon over hot pie.

Serve warm. Drizzle with additional caramel topping. Makes 8 servings.

PASTRY FOR A SINGLE-CRUST PIE: In a bowl stir together 1½ cups all-purpose flour and ¼ teaspoon salt. Using a pastry blender, cut in ½ cup shortening until pieces are peasize. Sprinkle 1 tablespoon cold water over part of the flour mixture; gently toss with a fork. Push moistened dough to side of the bowl. Repeat, using 1 tablespoon water at a time (4 to 5 tablespoons total), until flour mixture is moistened. Form dough into a ball. On a floured surface flatten dough with hands. Roll dough from center to edges to a 13-inch circle. To transfer pastry, wrap around rolling pin. Unroll pastry into a 9-inch deep-dish pie pan. Ease pastry into plate without stretching it. Trim pastry to 1 inch beyond edge of pie plate. Fold under extra pastry.

Garlic-Roasted Asparagus

Prep: 15 minutes   Roast: 10 minutes   Oven: 450°F

1½	pounds fresh asparagus spears
2	to 3 cloves garlic, thinly sliced
2	to 3 tablespoons olive oil
¼	teaspoon salt
¼	teaspoon black pepper

Preheat oven to 450°F. Snap off and discard woody bases from asparagus. Place asparagus and garlic in a 15×10×1-inch baking pan. Drizzle with oil and sprinkle with salt and pepper. Toss to coat.

Roast for 10 to 15 minutes or until asparagus is crisp-tender, stirring once halfway through roasting. Serve immediately. Makes 6 servings.

A single head
of garlic
offers flavor
enough for
many meals.

Gorgeous Garlic

Fragrant and pungent, hot and strong, garlic adds rich flavor to a variety of foods.

So popular, this edible bulb often gets top billing on recipes: garlic mashed potatoes, garlic bread, garlic chicken. This flavorful vegetable is used like an herb—as a seasoning. Roasted, garlic takes on a mild, nutty flavor and spreadable consistency. Use raw garlic in salad dressings and sauces to add unmistakable zip.

Garlic may get a bad rep for causing garlic breath, but it also has magical health benefits. The garlic family, which includes leeks, chives, shallots, and scallions, contains compounds that may reduce risks for cancer. Garlic is also a heart-healthy food because it helps to control high blood pressure and suppresses the harmful effects of low-density lipoprotein (LDL or bad) cholesterol. Wonder food indeed!

Garlic has been grown for thousands of years for its culinary and medicinal properties. It is a common ingredient in Mediterranean and Asian cuisines. Hardneck garlic is the hardiest form. Varieties in this group form cloves around a woody stem that sends up a curly flower stalk. Softneck garlic forms cloves around a soft neck or stem, which braids easily.

The typical lifespan of garlic (*Allium sativum*) is very different from most vegetables. First bulbs are planted in fall and harvested the following year. After planting the garlic bulbs, which look very much like tulip or daffodil bulbs, garlic sets roots and sits out the winter underground. In spring garlic sends up a shoot and may even start to bloom— tiny would-be flowers are called scapes. Remove them before the buds open to make the plant put more energy into the clove (for bigger and better harvests). Scapes have a mild garlic flavor and are edible—saute them in a little butter or olive oil for an early taste of what's to come.

Planting & Growing Tips

Remove the garlic scapes to put more of the plant's power into making a bigger bulb.

Separate the cloves from the bulb just before planting; don't separate them beforehand.

After planting garlic, spread a couple inches of mulch over the soil to help prevent injury to the plants from sudden cold spells in fall or spring. Mulch will also deter weeds in spring and help the soil conserve moisture.

Store garlic in a cool spot (lower than 40°F.) until you can use it. Properly cured garlic will usually hold for about 6 months.

harvest tip

If you're not sure when it's time to harvest bulbs, carefully dig up one bulb to check whether cloves are filling up the skin or wrappers. If plump, it's ready for harvest.

Garlic 101

SITE: Garlic prefers a spot in full sun and moist but well-drained soil.

BEDMATES: Rotate crops every year to prevent disease.

CARE: Garlic does well in lots of organic matter. Amend soil each year with lots of compost. Because garlic has a shallow root system, water well in spring, especially in May and June when the cloves are developing. Then stop watering in July to allow the foliage to die back before harvest. Garlic's small root system has a tough time competing with weeds. Mulch throughout the growing season and pull out any weeds as they pop up.

HOW TO START: Garlic is grown from the cloves. The larger the clove, the larger the bulb it produces. The best time to plant garlic is in the fall (even though many seed catalogs sell it in spring). Plant it right after your area's first killing frost (may be from late September to November or even December). After planting, garlic develops a root system in the cool soil; then it goes dormant over winter. The following spring garlic sends up leafy shoots. Plant individual garlic cloves about 1 inch deep and about 6 inches apart with the points up.

HARVEST: Midsummer, the leaves of garlic plants turn yellow and die back—a sign to get ready for harvest. Many gardeners wait to harvest until about half the leafy growth has turned brown—usually August or September. If ready, carefully dig up the bulbs. Try not to separate the cloves. Lift them out of the ground with a garden fork—don't yank them out of the ground by the leaves. Cut leaves back to 1 inch tall and brush off the soil to clean them. Leave garlic to dry in a warm spot for about 4 weeks to cure.

PESTS AND DISEASES: Garlic is generally very easy to grow, but there are several fungal issues that can affect crops. Garlic can also be damaged by nematodes, which are microscopic, and can't be seen on stems or leaves. Since most of the major diseases are found in the soil, yearly crop rotation of garlic beds helps produce healthy garlic. To avoid fungus, space plants to ensure good air circulation around stems and leaves.

recommended varieties

'NEW YORK WHITE' is also called 'Polish White'. It's a hardy, disease-resistant variety for northern regions.

'RUSSIAN RED' is a hardneck type with purple stripes on its cloves. It is exceptionally winter-hardy.

'SILVER WHITE' is a softneck type for warm climates. It produces easy-to-peel white bulbs.

'SPANISH ROJA' is a hardneck type with medium-hot flavor. The brown-skin cloves are excellent for roasting.

Herbed Garlic Bread

Prep: 15 minutes   Bake: 15 minutes
Oven: 375°F

½	cup butter, softened
2	tablespoons snipped fresh Italian (flat-leaf) parsley
1½	teaspoons minced garlic (about 3 cloves)
¾	teaspoon kosher salt or ½ teaspoon salt
	Dash black pepper
1	14- to 18-ounce baguette or Italian bread

Preheat oven to 375°F. In a small bowl combine butter, parsley, garlic, salt, and a dash pepper.

Without cutting through the bottom crust, slice baguette in 1½-inch slices. Generously spread butter mixture between slices. Wrap baguette in heavy foil. Bake 15 minutes or until heated through. Serve warm. Makes 10 to 12 slices.

Garlic Mashed Potatoes and Parsnips

Prep: 35 minutes   Bake: 20 minutes
Oven: 350°F

3	pounds baking potatoes, such as Russet (5 to 6 large)
1½	pounds parsnips
1	head garlic
2	teaspoons olive oil
¾	cup milk
½	cup butter
¾	teaspoon salt
⅛	teaspoon freshly ground black pepper

Peel potatoes and parsnips; cut into ½-inch chunks. In a covered Dutch oven or large saucepan cook potatoes and parsnips for 25 minutes in enough boiling salted water to cover; drain.

Meanwhile, preheat oven to 350°F. Peel away the dry outer layers of skin from the garlic head, leaving skins and cloves intact. Cut off and discard about ½ inch off the pointed top portion of the garlic head. Place garlic, cut side up, in a custard cup. Drizzle with olive oil. Cover with foil and bake about 20 minutes or until garlic is tender when pierced with the tip of a sharp knife. Cool. Press garlic pulp from each clove with your fingers and place in custard cup; mash with a fork. Set aside.

Mash potatoes and parsnips with a potato masher or ricer or beat with a mixer on low. In a small saucepan combine milk and butter. Bring just to boiling. Stir milk mixture into potato mixture. Stir in mashed garlic pulp, salt, and pepper. Heat through. Makes 14 servings.

Honey-Glazed Onions
Start to Finish: 25 minutes

2	**cups fresh or frozen small whole onions**
2	**tablespoons honey**
2	**tablespoons white wine vinegar**
1	**tablespoon snipped fresh basil or 1 teaspoon dried basil, crushed**
¼	**teaspoon ground sage**

If using fresh onions, in a medium covered saucepan cook onions in a small amount of boiling water for 8 to 10 minutes or just until tender; drain in colander. Cool slightly; peel. (Or cook frozen onions according to package directions; drain in colander.)

In the same saucepan combine honey, vinegar, basil, and sage. Add onions. Cook and stir until onions are glazed and heated through. Makes 4 servings.

The sharp, hot flavor of onions adds a blast to sandwiches and salads. To sample the sweet side of onions, cook them.

Earthy Onions

Like bit players in the major drama of many meals, onions are sauteed into soups and stews, caramelized with sweet butter, spooned on vegetables or meat dishes, or chopped fresh for salads. And while cutting up a raw onion may make you cry, onions remain one of the fastest, simplest, and least expensive foods to flavor savory dishes. Hint: Rinse onions in water or freeze them for a few minutes before cutting or slicing to prevent the release of sulfuric compound, which causes eyes to tear.

Growing onions in the garden is so easy—and such a treat. Fresh onions—scallions and green onions—are ready in spring, harvested straight from the garden. (See more about these onions on page 68.) Large onions, sometimes called storage onions, need time—up to 110 days—to grow. When you harvest the juicy bulbs in mid to late summer, they've gained heft and flavor from growing subterraneanly. Enjoy them well into winter.

With so many varieties of onions to choose from—in yellow, white, and red—you may want to plant several types to see which you like best. Onions offer a wide range of flavors. Yellow onions have a hot, complex flavor due to high sulfur levels (the reason for tearing when you cut into them). Yellow onions saute to a rich brown and sweeten when cooked. Because they are strong, eating yellow onions raw is an acquired taste. The mild and sweet 'Vidalia', 'Walla Walla', and 'Maui' onions have higher water contents and can be eaten raw by the slice or develop extra flavor when grilled. Red onions are sweet enough to eat raw; they offer splashes of bright color to potato or other vegetable salads. White onions have a clean, tangy taste; chop them and toss them into salads, onto guacamole, and over tacos.

Onions are part of the large and diverse *Allium* genus of pungent edibles such as chives, shallots, scallions, and garlic as well as inedible garden flowers such as the purple-flower *Allium gigantium*. The edible onion is *Allium cepa*. Sometimes called small onions, shallots are small, more garlicky, and best cooked in sauces or sautes. Many people find them too hot to dice and eat raw.

Planting & Growing Tips

To ensure the largest and tastiest harvests, plant onions early in the season.

Short-rooted shallots are easy to harvest—give them a tug and they pop right out of the ground.

Grow onions in containers. Just poke seedlings around other veggies.

Grow specific onion varieties suited specifically to your region. Grow long-day types in the North and short-day types in the South. Or plant intermediate-day types anywhere.

Onions need to cure for a few days after digging them up. Lay out onions in a warm, airy spot. When the outer skin becomes papery and crispy dry, the onions have cured.

harvest tip

Onions are mature and ready to harvest in mid to late summer. Watch for the green plant top to start to wither and turn brown—the foliage may collapse onto the ground. Don't allow mature onions to sit in wet soil—they rot rapidly.

recommended varieties

ONIONS

'CANDY HYBRID' is a mild-flavor yellow intermediate-day onion. It stores fairly well. 85 days.

'COPRA HYBRID' is a widely adapted long-day yellow storage onion that matures in 105 days. It is sweeter than most other storage onions.

'GIANT RED HAMBURGER' bears dark red bulbs that are good for slicing. The interior flesh is white and sweet. It is best adapted to the South. 95 days.

'REDWING HYBRID' has pungent, red-flesh bulbs that store well. It's ready to harvest 110 days after planting.

'SUPERSTAR HYBRID' produces huge white bulbs that weigh up to 1 pound. It is day neutral, so can be planted anywhere. 100 days.

SHALLOTS

'AMBITION' shallot produces divided bulbs with reddish-copper skin and white flesh. 90 days.

'GOLDEN GOURMET' is a mild-tasting, high-yielding shallot that keeps well. 77 days.

Onions 101

SITE: Onions prefer to grow in a sunny spot in well-drained soil.

BEDMATES: Plant onions with carrots, leeks, beets, kohlrabi, strawberries, Brassicas (broccoli, cauliflower, kale), dill, lettuce, and tomatoes.

CARE: Take care when weeding around young onions. Hand-weeding is best because onions have shallow root systems; cultivating tools may harm bulbs. Keep well watered, but not too wet. Side-dress with fertilizer.

HOW TO START: Grow onions from sets, transplants, or seeds. The fastest way to raise onions is to plant sets. Dried-looking little onion seedlings can be purchased in bundles and planted directly in the garden. Or sow onion seeds indoors in flats in early spring; when the seedlings are 4 inches tall, transplant them into beds.

HARVEST: When onion foliage begins to die back naturally, stop watering the plants. About a week later, pull the bulbs out of the ground. Onions need to cure for a few days. Choose a warm, airy spot and lay harvested onions on a layer of newspapers or a screen. When the outer skin becomes papery and crispy dry, the onions have cured. If you like, braid the tops together and make attractive onion bundles. Or cut off the foliage, leaving a 1-inch stub above the bulb. Either hang up onion bunches or place them in mesh bags. Store in a cool, dry place (50°F to 60°F). Onions will last for several months. Harvest shallots after side bulbs have formed and the tops have begun to dry. Separate the side bulbs, dry them, and store as you would onions.

PESTS AND DISEASES: Onions can get a number of diseases, most of which are caused by prolonged wet conditions. Some fungus species affect onions: leaf blight (also known as blast), which has white or gold specks on the leaves and can cause crop failure; leaf fleck, which causes only surface leaf damage; and neck rot, which affects stored onions.

Beef, Mushroom, and Onion Tart

Start to Finish: 30 minutes   Oven: 425°F

12 ounces lean ground beef
1 8-ounce package sliced mushrooms
½ of a medium red onion, cut into thin wedges
¼ teaspoon salt
¼ teaspoon black pepper
1 13.8-ounce package refrigerated pizza dough
3 ounces blue cheese, crumbled
   Fresh oregano and/or pizza seasoning (optional)

Heat oven to 425°F. In a large skillet cook beef, mushrooms, and onion on medium heat about 8 minutes or until beef is browned and onion is tender, stirring occasionally. Drain off fat. Stir in salt and pepper.

Meanwhile, grease a large baking sheet or line with parchment paper. Unroll pizza dough on baking sheet Roll or pat dough to a 15×12-inch rectangle. Top dough with beef mixture, keeping filling within 1½ inches of all edges. Fold edges over the filling, pleating as needed.

Bake tart 15 minutes or until crust is golden. Top with blue cheese and, if desired, oregano and/or pizza seasoning. Makes 4 servings.

Caramelized Onion Soup
Prep: 25 minutes   Cook: 30 minutes   Broil: 2 minutes

3	pounds sweet onions, such as Vidalia, Walla Walla, or Maui
3	tablespoons olive oil, margarine, or butter
12	medium shallots, halved (about 12 ounces)
4	cups beef broth or reduced-sodium chicken broth
2	tablespoons dry white wine (optional)
	Salt and black pepper
6	½-inch-thick slices sourdough or French bread (4 ounces)
6	ounces Gouda or Edam cheese, thinly sliced
	Green onion tops (optional)

Cut about ½ inch off the tops of 3 of the whole onions. Peel off the papery outer leaves. Trim the root ends, but leave them intact. Turn 1 onion to rest on its top. Cut 2 thin (about ¼-inch) slices from the center of the onion, cutting down from the root end to the onion top. Be careful to keep slices intact. Repeat with remaining 2 onions for a total of 6 thin center-cut onion slices. Set aside remaining onions.

In a large skillet heat 1 tablespoon of the oil. Carefully add the 6 onion slices in a single layer. Cook, uncovered, on medium heat for 3 to 4 minutes or until golden brown. Turn carefully with a wide metal spatula. Cook about 3 minutes more or until golden brown on second side. Carefully remove from skillet and drain on paper towels.

Thinly slice remaining onion portions. Halve and cut remaining whole onions into thin slices. You should have 6 to 7 cups onion slices. In a 4- or 4½-quart Dutch oven heat the remaining 2 tablespoons oil on medium heat. Stir in the sliced onions and halved shallots. Cook, uncovered, on medium heat for 20 to 25 minutes or until onions are tender, stirring occasionally. Increase heat to medium-high and cook 5 minutes or until onions are golden brown, stirring occasionally.

Stir broth and wine, if using, into onions in Dutch oven. Heat through. Season to taste with a little salt and pepper.

Meanwhile, place bread slices on rack of broiler pan. Broil about 4 inches from the heat for 1 minute or until lightly toasted. Turn bread over; top each piece with a slice of cheese. Broil for 1 to 2 minutes or until cheese just begins to melt.

To serve, ladle soup into bowls. Top each with a piece of cheese toast. Add a caramelized onion slice and green onion tops. Makes about 7 cups (6 main-dish servings).

Brussels Sprouts with Lemon Sauce
Start to Finish: 20 minutes

3	cups Brussels sprouts (12 ounce)
¾	cup chicken broth
1	teaspoon butter
1	clove garlic, minced
2	tablespoons chicken broth
1½	teaspoons cornstarch
½	teaspoon finely shredded lemon peel
1	tablespoon lemon juice
⅛	teaspoon black pepper
2	teaspoons snipped fresh dillweed

Trim Brussels sprouts stems and remove any wilted outer leaves.

In a medium saucepan combine sprouts, the ¾ cup broth, butter, and garlic. Bring to boiling; reduce heat. Simmer, covered, for 7 to 10 minutes or until sprouts are crisp-tender. Using a slotted spoon, transfer sprouts to a serving bowl. Keep warm.

Meanwhile, in a small bowl combine the 2 tablespoons chicken broth, the cornstarch, lemon peel, lemon juice, and pepper. Gradually add lemon mixture to hot broth in saucepan. Cook and stir on medium heat until mixture is thickened and bubbly. Cook and stir for 2 minutes more. Stir in fresh dillweed.

Pour lemon sauce over sprouts. Makes 6 side-dish servings.

This other-worldly-looking vegetable produces meal after meal of delightfully sweet sprouts.

Amazing Brussels Sprouts

If you're a fan of Brussels sprouts

but have yet to raise them or see them growing, you are in for a surprise. They don't look or grow like any other vegetable. Brussels sprout plants have thick, trunklike stalks that grow 2 to 3 feet tall. They look like little trees.

The round, cabbagelike sprouts grow up the stalk, studding the entire length. Each stalk can produce 50 to 100 sprouts. In short, Brussels sprouts are a showstopper in the garden. And if you have kids, you should add a couple Brussels sprouts plants to your vegetable garden if only for the surprise factor. Kids love to harvest these little cabbages, which are easy to pluck off the massive stem.

Anther reason to grow Brussels sprouts is that they are one of the last crops to harvest from the garden. You can have freshly harvested sprouts for Thanksgiving!

Although garden-variety Brussels sprouts are generally smaller than those sold in stores, homegrown sprouts have a sweeter, more nutty flavor. They are a slow-growing vegetable—it takes 90 days or more to reach maturity. Plan to wait until after a few frosts to harvest—a cold snap enhances the flavor, making them milder and sweeter. In mild areas, or if there is a deep snow cover, you may be able to harvest Brussels sprouts all winter.

Brussels sprouts (*Brassica oleracea Gemmifera* group) are members of the cabbage family and have all the health benefits attributed to this group of vegetables. Cruciferous vegetables, according to current research, may offer protection against some forms of cancer. Unlike most green vegetables, Brussels sprouts are also a protein source as well as a good source of fiber and vitamin C.

Planting & Growing Tips

Sow or transplant seedlings; space plants 24 to 36 inches apart.

To make Brussels sprouts mature more quickly, remove the growing tip on the top of the plant when the sprouts at the bottom of the stem measure about ½ inch in diameter; harvest sprouts 2 weeks later.

Harvest lowest sprouts first; keep harvesting up the stem. Harvest sprouts before the leaves yellow.

Brussels Sprouts 101

SITE: Like most vegetables, Brussels sprouts require a sunny spot, but will grow with a little shade.

BEDMATES: Plant with members of the same family: broccoli, cauliflower, and kale.

CARE: Easy-care Brussels sprouts need little more than sunshine and regular water to flourish. Keep beds clean of weeds; pull weeds by hand to avoid damaging the roots or stem. Mulch with compost.

HOW TO START: Because Brussels sprouts take so long to mature, consider starting seeds indoors in early spring. Plant seeds ½ inch deep and 2 inches apart in a seed-starting tray about 90 days before the first frost date. In spring transplant seedlings directly into the garden.

HARVEST: Pick sprouts from the base of the plant upward. Start harvesting when sprouts are about 1 to 1½ inches in diameter.

PESTS AND DISEASES: Brussels sprouts are long-growing, offering lots of opportunity for pest infestation. Repel cutworm damage by adding a cutworm collar around seedlings. Remove aphids with a blast from the garden hose. The biggest pest, however, is cabbage worms. Remove cabbage loopers by hand or use Bt. Control harlequin bugs and flea beetles with appropriate insecticides. Prevent cabbage maggot with diatomaceous earth. And control clubroot and black rot through crop rotation.

recommended varieties

'JADE CROSS E HYBRID' is an improvement over the old 'Jade Cross Hybrid,' incorporating tolerance of botrytis, a fungal disease, into its characteristics. It matures early and bears dark green sprouts.

'RED RUBINE' is an heirloom variety with purplish red sprouts that hold their color even after cooking. It is an attractive alternative to common green varieties.

'BUBBLES' produces round 2-inch flavorful sprouts. Tolerates heat and drought conditions. Harvest 82 days after planting.

'OLIVER' is one of the earliest to harvest Brussels sprouts. It has colorful red, purple, and white leaves with ruffled edges.

Mustard-Glazed Brussels Sprouts and Oranges

Start to Finish: 25 minutes

- **3   medium oranges (such as blood and/or navel)**
- **1   pound fresh Brussels sprouts (about 4 cups)**
- **1   tablespoon margarine or butter**
- **2   teaspoons cornstarch**
- **¼   teaspoon five-spice powder or dried dillweed**
- **2   tablespoons honey-mustard**

Finely shred enough peel from 1 orange to make ½ teaspoon peel; set aside. Halve orange; squeeze juice. Working over a bowl to catch the juices, peel and section the remaining oranges; set aside. Combine the juices to equal ⅓ cup (add water, if necessary).

Rinse Brussels sprouts. Halve any large sprouts. In a medium saucepan cook sprouts, uncovered, in a small amount of boiling water for 10 to 12 minutes or until tender. Drain and transfer to a serving bowl. Gently stir in orange sections; cover and keep warm.

In the same saucepan melt margarine or butter. Stir in cornstarch and five-spice powder or dillweed. Stir in reserved orange peel, orange juice, and mustard. Cook and stir until thickened and bubbly. Cook and stir for 1 minute more. Transfer sprouts and fruit to serving bowl. Top with sauce; toss to serve. Makes 5 or 6 side-dish servings.

Creamy Brussels Sprouts

Prep: 15 minutes   Cook: 12 minutes
Bake: 20 minutes   Oven: 350°F

	Nonstick cooking spray
1	**medium onion, quartered and thinly sliced**
3	**cloves garlic, minced**
3	**tablespoons butter**
2	**pounds Brussels sprouts, trimmed and halved, or green beans, trimmed**
1	**teaspoon snipped fresh thyme or ¼ teaspoon dried thyme, crushed**
¾	**cup reduced-sodium chicken broth**
¾	**cup whipping cream**
¼	**teaspoon ground nutmeg**
½	**cup finely shredded Parmesan cheese or Pecorino Romano cheese**
¼	**teaspoon salt**
⅛	**teaspoon black pepper**

Preheat oven to 350°F. Lightly coat a 1½-quart oval gratin baking dish or baking dish with nonstick cooking spray.

In a large skillet cook onion and garlic in butter over medium heat for 3 minutes or until softened. Stir in sprouts and thyme. Cook for 4 minutes or until onions begin to brown. Add broth. Bring to boiling. Cook, stirring occasionally, for 3 to 4 minutes or until broth is nearly evaporated. Add whipping cream and nutmeg. Cook 4 minutes or until mixture begins to thicken. Transfer to baking dish. Stir in half the cheese and all the salt and pepper. Sprinkle with remaining cheese.

Bake, uncovered, 20 to 25 minutes or until sprouts are tender. Makes 8 to 10 servings.

Preserving

A successful growing season means big yields. When you can't serve everything fresh and want to put aside a taste of summer for cooler months, preserving is the way to go. Freezing, canning, and drying the fruits of your labors is cost-effective and satisfying.

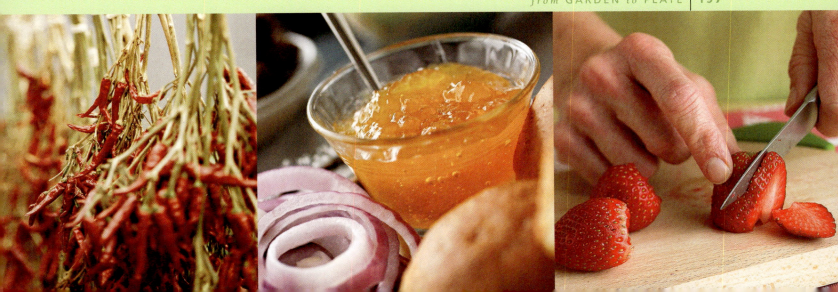

What's Fresh?

FOR CANNING OR FREEZING, USE THE FRESHEST IN-SEASON FRUITS AND VEGETABLES FROM YOUR GARDEN OR LOCAL FARMERS' MARKETS. HERE'S WHEN TO EXPECT THE MOST AVAILABLE PRODUCE.

APRIL

AVAILABLE BUT IN SMALL SUPPLY:
asparagus, green beans, rhubarb

MAY

HIGHLY AVAILABLE; CAN OR FREEZE NOW:
asparagus, green beans, rhubarb

AVAILABLE MIDSEASON:
green beans

AVAILABLE BUT IN SMALL SUPPLY:
lima beans, beets, cabbage, cauliflower, cucumbers (pickling), onions, peppers, apricots, blackberries, raspberries

JUNE

HIGHLY AVAILABLE; CAN OR FREEZE NOW:
asparagus, green beans, cabbage, cucumbers (pickling), peas, blueberries, rhubarb, strawberries

AVAILABLE MIDSEASON:
lima beans, beets, cauliflower, corn, onions, tomatoes, apricots, blackberries, currants, gooseberries, nectarines, peaches, raspberries

AVAILABLE BUT IN SMALL SUPPLY:
peppers, apples, cherries, plums

JULY

HIGHLY AVAILABLE; CAN OR FREEZE NOW:
lima beans, green beans, beets, cabbage, cauliflower, corn, cucumbers (pickling), onions, peas, tomatoes, apricots, blackberries, blueberries, cherries, currants, gooseberries, nectarines, peaches, raspberries

AVAILABLE MIDSEASON:
peppers, apples, plums, rhubarb, strawberries

AUGUST

HIGHLY AVAILABLE; CAN OR FREEZE NOW:
lima beans, beets, cabbage, cauliflower, corn, cucumbers (pickling), onions, peppers, tomatoes, apples, apricots, blackberries, blueberries, nectarines, peaches, pears, plums

AVAILABLE MIDSEASON:
green beans, cherries, raspberries

AVAILABLE BUT IN SMALL SUPPLY:
peas, currants, gooseberries, grapes (Concord), rhubarb, strawberries

SEPTEMBER

HIGHLY AVAILABLE; CAN OR FREEZE NOW:
lima beans, cabbage, cauliflower, onions, tomatoes, apples, grapes (Concord), pears, plums

AVAILABLE MIDSEASON:
beets, corn, cucumbers (pickling), peppers, peaches

AVAILABLE BUT IN SMALL SUPPLY:
peas, apricots, blackberries, blueberries, cherries, nectarines, raspberries

Know Your Produce

Not all tomatoes are created equal. Or cucumbers. Even grapes. Understand key differences among fruits and vegetables to make sure canning projects turn out perfectly.

Undamaged and unblemished

When you put top-quality produce in a jar, you get top-quality food from it. Use produce within a day or two of harvesting or purchasing. Store in the refrigerator if necessary (except for tomatoes). Discard produce that is diseased, moldy, or insect-damaged, though you can cut out small bruises and spots.

Sweetness and ripeness

Choose produce that is moderately ripe. Avoid fruit that is overripe or underripe (with the exception of recipes that specify, say, green tomatoes). Fully ripe yet firm fruit has the best, fullest flavor and processes the best. In some cases recipes specify the ripeness of the fruit—it's that critical. Berries and fruits at the peak of their flavor will mash to the correct consistency and produce the most delicious jams and jellies. Underripe or inferior berries have less flavor and less-than-ideal texture.

Acidity

Some fruits and vegetables have higher acid levels than others. Acidic produce is naturally easier to preserve because acid inhibits the growth of some microorganisms. This is the reason that many home canning recipes rely on vinegar—it's very acidic. Other recipes call for a small amount of lemon juice to boost acidity.

Pectin

This natural substance occurs in a variety of fruits and is the substance that causes jams and jellies to gel. Most recipes call for the addition of pectin, but some fruits, such as gooseberries, naturally have so much pectin that adding more isn't necessary. Underripe fruit is high in pectin; overly ripe fruit is low in pectin. Making preserves with overripe fruit might result in a runny product. Because the sugar in each recipe interacts with the pectin, do not alter the amount of sugar. If you want low- or no-sugar jams and jellies, follow low- or no-sugar recipes.

The right type of produce

Some varieties or cultivars of produce process better than others, and with better results. Paste-type tomatoes, sometimes called roma or plum tomatoes, are firmer and meatier with fewer seeds and juice than beefsteak or slicing tomatoes. Pickling cucumbers, sometimes called Kirby cucumbers, are firmer and stand up to the brining process better, remaining crisp. Avoid wax coating on produce—it prevents absorption of liquids. Grapes have varying flavors, juiciness, and pectin levels. Use the grape specified in a recipe whenever possible.

How to Prep Produce

Before making pickles, preserves, or any other type of canned or frozen produce, simple produce preparation is necessary. Here's how to professionally prep even large amounts of fruits and vegetables.

Picking

For freezing or canning, use only produce that is at its peak of ripeness and flavor. Farmer's market produce and homegrown fruits and veggies should be processed within a few days. For example, pickling cucumbers and raspberries have short shelf lives and can wither or mildew in just a day or two.

Washing

Use only water, rinsing thoroughly in a large colander. Washing removes dirt, insects, and bacteria. Use a scrub brush to get dirt off rough root vegetables such as carrots.

Blanching

Some recipes specify blanching—simply putting produce into rapidly boiling water for a short time, usually a minute or two. Blanching, most often called for in freezer recipes, further cleans produce and kills some organisms on the surface. It also slows or stops the action of enzymes, which causes loss of flavor, color, and texture. Blanching also helps preserve color and vitamin content.

Peeling

For tomatoes, peaches, and other soft-flesh produce, blanching makes peeling easy. Hot water heats and softens the flesh right beneath the skin. Plunging the produce in cold water causes steam, which cools and leaves tiny air pockets that allow the skin to slip off easily. But only peel when the recipe specifies it. Some peels are left on because they contain valuable pectin, which helps thicken the product. In other cases the peel helps to keep the produce intact.

How to Peel Peaches and Tomatoes
BLANCHING PRODUCE LOOSENS THE SKIN, MAKING PEELING A SNAP.

1 Bring a large pan of water to boiling. Add the produce and leave in for 30 to 60 seconds or until skins start to split.

2 Remove and plunge produce into a large bowl of ice water. Remove from the cold water after a few minutes. Use a knife to easily pull off the skin.

Prep Guide 101

TOMATOES
Make an X at the blossom end of a tomato, then blanch. The X encourages the tomato skin to split so you can slip off the skin easily with your fingers.

STRAWBERRIES
Cut out the stem end of strawberries. This process is called hulling.

APPLES
Make processing apples a breeze by investing a few dollars in an apple corer. Simply push it firmly into the apple, twist, and pull.

Food Preservation Methods

Once you have your hands on all that delicious produce, you'll find several ways to preserve its goodness. Choose the right method to produce the best results.

BOILING-WATER CANNING

The method used to process produce depends on the desired result. Should raspberries be made into a rich jam, frozen, or elegantly brandied? Should tomatoes be made into a rich sauce, frozen whole, or dried? Here's an overview of basic processing methods.

Boiling-water canning

A boiling-water canner is simply a very large pot with a rack in the bottom and a lid on the top. Jars are submerged in boiling water for a specified time. They are heated to a temperature of 212°F. This method is used mainly for fruits, pickles, salsa, and other high-acid foods. It's also used for some tomato recipes.

Pressure canning

A pressure canner has a lid that locks on and a dial that allows you to regulate the steam pressure building up inside by turning the burner heat up or down. Pressurized steam is much hotter than boiling water—pressure canning heats jars to 240°F. This higher heat kills tougher microorganisms that can thrive in low-acid foods, such as green beans, soups, and sauces with meat.

Freezing

An easy way to preserve garden produce, freezing preserves texture in a way that canning doesn't. Freezing is also easy—just put food into airtight containers or bags, remove excess air, and stash in the freezer!

Brining

Merely by marinating some foods in a vinegar-base brine you can preserve them for weeks longer than they would otherwise stay fresh. Simply make the brine, pack into scrupulously clean containers, and store in the refrigerator up to the maximum recommended time.

Preserving in alcohol

Alcohol, a disinfectant, kills many harmful bacteria. You can preserve fruit in nothing but alcohol, but it's more flavorful to add spices and other flavorings.

Drying

Food dries most reliably in a dehydrator, a small electric countertop appliance. You can also dry foods in the oven with some success, as with dried tomatoes and apples, which intensifies flavor and alters texture. Food dried in a dehydrator can be safely stored in plastic bags or jars on a shelf. However, food dried in an oven doesn't dehydrate as completely, so it should be stored in plastic bags in the refrigerator.

PRESSURE CANNING

FREEZING

BRINING

PRESERVING IN ALCOHOL

DRYING

Canning Basics
Stock your pantry with home-canned pickles, preserves, jams and jellies, adding summer freshness and flavor to your table all year long.

Imagine pulling a jar of tomatoes out of your pantry and opening up to the taste of last summer's garden. That's what you can have when you can your extra produce.

Decades ago people canned because they had to. Putting up food in crocks and jars was one of the most reliable ways to preserve the bounty of the summer garden.

Today people can because they choose to. They have more control over how the foods are grown and processed—and few things are more satisfying than stepping back from a canning session to admire gleaming jars filled with gorgeous produce.

Over the years the basic process of canning remains the same, however: Heat food to a specified temperature for a particular period of time to destroy harmful microorganisms and to inactivate enzymes. The process also vacuum-seals jars to remove air and prevent other microorganisms from invading.

Microorganisms include molds, yeasts, and bacteria, naturally occurring and sometimes even beneficial, such as those found in yogurt. But others are harmful and must be destroyed with heat.

Enzymes are also naturally occurring and helpful in nature. But in canning, enzymes can affect the color, texture, and flavor of foods. Heating inactivates these enzymes.

The vacuum seal is a result of heat penetrating the jar in the canner. As food and air in the jar expand with heat, pressure builds in the jar.

After the jars are removed from the canner to cool on the counter, the air cools and contracts, creating a vacuum in the jar, pulling the lid downward into a concave shape. (Metal lids make a popping sound as this happens.) The sticky compound around the rim of the lid, softened by the heat, cools and seals the jar. The result? A shelf-stable product that can be stored in a pantry or cupboard to enjoy up to 1 year.

THE FIVE RULES OF CANNING

1 Know which canner to use
The boiling-water canner—basically a big pot with a lid and a rack in the bottom—is used for high-acid foods, which naturally resist bacteria growth. Pressure canners, used with low-acid foods and recipes that are especially prone to harboring harmful microorganisms, heat food hotter than boiling-water canners. Recipes will specify which type of canner is appropriate.

2 Choose the right jars
Use jars made specifically for canning. Don't use glass jars from purchased food, even if they look like canning jars. Don't use jars that look different from the canning jars currently on the market. And avoid jars with chipped edges, which can affect the seal. Use the size jar specified in the recipe because it takes longer to achieve the critical internal temperature in larger jars.

3 Use lids properly
Use the special two-piece lids manufactured for canning. Reuse the rings, but do not reuse the lids, which have a special sticky compound that seals the jar. Don't screw lids on too tightly or they won't create a vacuum seal properly. Heat the lids in very hot but not boiling water or the compound won't seal. Test for sealing on each jar after it has cooled. Press the center of the lid; if the button is depressed and does not make a popping sound, it has sealed properly.

4 Choose the right recipe
Modern canning recipes are safer than those from just 20 years ago. Jellies, for example, are no longer sealed with wax but in vacuum-sealed jars. Foods may be processed longer or hotter. Always use tested recipes from reliable, current sources—and follow the recipes exactly. Don't alter ingredients. Alterations can change the acidity and compromise food safety.

5 Keep it clean and keep it hot
Keep everything scrupulously clean. Wash and sterilize jars. Pack hot food into hot jars one at a time—not assembly-line style.

MEASURING HEADSPACE

The amount of headspace is specified by each recipe and is important to ensure that each jar seals properly.

Measure headspace with a ruler or canning tool from the top of the jar to the top of the liquid. It's okay if a little bit of solid food rises above the liquid; it will settle into the liquid over time.

¼"
½"
1"

Boiling-Water Canning

This method is the simpler of the two. Prepare the food and put it in the jars, then submerge in boiling water for the specified time. Tomatoes are shown here, but overall steps are the same for other foods.

1 PREPARE JARS AND LIDS

While you're preparing the food to be canned, heat water in the canner. Fill the canner about halfway with water and position the rack. Set jars in the canner to sterilize.

DIP THE JARS You can simply dip the jars in a large pan of simmering water for a few minutes and then load then, still hot, with food.

HEAT THE LIDS Lids can be heated in hot (not boiling) water right in the canner. Lift out with a magnetic canning lid wand or tongs.

2 PREPARE THE FOOD

Select, wash, and cut up produce.

SCORE THE TOMATOES Make an X in the blossom end of each tomato with a small sharp knife.

BLANCH Heat a large kettle of water to boiling. Drop in the tomatoes to simmer for 30 seconds.

COOL AND PEEL Immediately plunge the tomatoes into icy water to loosen the skins. The skins will slip off easily.

3 FILL THE JARS

The cold-pack method for tomatoes is shown here. Follow the exact process specified in your recipe.

PACK the jar as tightly as you can with the food without crushing it. Top with any hot liquid as specified in the recipe.

REMOVE AIR BUBBLES by inserting a special canning tool or a thin, flexible spatula down along the sides of the jar to remove any air bubbles. Measure headspace, adding or removing liquid as needed.

WIPE rim and threads of jar with a clean, damp cloth to remove any residue that might interfere with the seal.

PUT ON LID by setting lid on jar and screwing on band no more than fingertip-tight, just tight enough that you could turn the band another ¼ to ½ inch tighter. This is important for a proper seal.

4 PROCESS THE JARS

Submerging the jars in boiling water heats and sterilizes the food inside and is the first step in creating a sealed jar.

PLACE JARS IN CANNER as you fill each jar. Set it back in the canner filled with simmering water. The canner shown has a rack with handles to hang on the canner rim so jars sit halfway in the water.

PROCESS JARS When all jars are filled, lower them into the canner. They should be covered with 1 to 2 inches water. Add more boiling water if needed to achieve this. Start processing time from the moment the water starts to boil. Keep at a low, rolling boil.

REMOVE JARS When the processing time is up, turn off heat. Using pot holders, lift up the rack and rest handles on the side of the canner. Allow the jars to cool in place for a few minutes.

5 COOL

SET JARS on a wire rack or towel on a countertop (cold, bare countertops can crack jars). Do not tighten bands. Allow to cool 12 to 24 hours. After that time, test the seal by firmly pressing your finger on the center of the lid. It should not give. If it makes a popping sound, it is not properly sealed. Store unsealed food in the refrigerator and eat the food soon. Otherwise, store sealed jars in a cool, dry place up to 1 year.

Pressure Canning

Some foods are low acid and require the more intense heat created in a pressure canner. Green beans are one such food, but the steps shown here are the same as for other pressure-canned foods.

1 PREPARE JARS AND LIDS

While you prepare the food, heat 2 or 3 inches of water in the pressure canner with the lid set on it loosely. Set the jars in the canner to sterilize, but do not lock the lid in place or pressure will start to build.

2 PREPARE THE FOOD

Select, wash, and cut up produce.

WASH AND TRIM Then cut off and discard any woody stems. Cut off the entire tail end of the bean, if desired, but it's not necessary.

CUT THE BEANS Cut or snip the beans into bite-size sections. Short pieces will fit into the jar more easily and make them easy to eat.

3 FILL THE JARS

The hot-pack method is shown, but the process is similar for pressure-canning.

FILL JARS with produce. Remove one jar at a time from the canner. Fill with food, using a funnel as needed to keep jar rims clean. Pack in produce with your fingers as tightly as you can without crushing it. Fill one hot sterilized jar at a time; do not fill a cooled jar.

ADD HOT LIQUID Top with boiling water, brine, or other hot liquid as specified in the recipe. Measure headspace (see page 207). Add or remove liquid as needed.

REMOVE AIR BUBBLES Use a thin, flexible spatula or canning tool to remove air bubbles. Add more water if needed to achieve the correct headspace.

PUT ON LID Wipe off the jar rim and threads with a clean cloth. Set lid in place and screw band on fingertip-tight, just ¼ to ½ inch from very tight. This is important so air can escape for a proper seal. Place the jar back in the canner before filling the next jar.

4 PROCESS THE JARS

When jars are filled, close the canner and allow pressure to build, following canner-specific directions.

FILL THE CANNER Set the last jar in place. Water in the canner should be only a few inches up and not cover jars. Only enough water to create steam is needed.

LOCK THE LID Set lid in place and twist so handles lock in place.

VENT THE CANNER Turn heat to high and allow a full head of steam to come out of the vent pipe. Allow to vent for 10 minutes. Adjust weights on the pressure regulator as specified in the recipe. Set the pressure regulator on the vent pipe to plug it.

ACHIEVE THE CORRECT PRESSURE The safety valve pops from down to up position, showing the canner is pressurized. Do not open the canner. When the pressure regulator starts to rock, adjust heat so it makes a steady rattling sound. Set the timer for the time specified in the recipe.

5 COOL THE JARS

Once processing is complete, allow the canner to depressurize, then cool the jars.

DEPRESSURIZE When the timer goes off, turn off the heat. Do not open the lid. Wait until the safety valve drops back down to show that the canner is no longer pressurized and is safe to open.

OPEN THE CANNER Remove the pressure regulator. (Very little or no steam should escape.) Unlock the handles and open the canner away from you so steam is directed away from you.

COOL THE JARS Allow jars to stand in the canner for 10 minutes to cool slightly. Remove them from the canner and set on a wire rack or dry towel on a countertop. Do not tighten lids. Allow to cool for 12 to 24 hours. Test seals by pressing on the lid (it should not pop up or down). Refrigerate any improperly sealed food to eat soon. Store others in a cool, dry place.

Freezing Vegetables

ASPARAGUS

PREPARATION: Allow 2½ to 4½ pounds per quart. Wash; scrape off scales. Break off woody bases where spears snap easily. Wash again. Sort by thickness. Leave whole or cut into 1-inch lengths.

HOW TO FREEZE: Blanch small spears for 2 minutes and large for 4 minutes; cool quickly. Fill containers; shake down, leaving no headspace.

BEANS: BUTTER, LIMA, OR PINTO

PREPARATION: Allow 3 to 5 pounds unshelled beans per quart. Wash, shell, rinse, drain, and sort beans by size.

HOW TO FREEZE: Blanch small beans for 2 minutes, medium beans for 3 minutes, and large beans for 4 minutes; cool quickly. Fill containers loosely, leaving a ½-inch headspace.

BEANS: GREEN, WAX, SNAP, OR ITALIAN

PREPARATION: Allow 1½ to 2½ pounds per quart. Wash; remove ends and strings. Leave whole or cut into 1-inch pieces.

HOW TO FREEZE: Blanch for 3 minutes; cool quickly. Fill containers; shake down, leaving a ½-inch headspace.

PEAS, EDIBLE PODS

PREPARATION: Wash Chinese, snow, sugar, or sugar snap peas. Remove stems, blossom ends, and any strings.

HOW TO FREEZE: Blanch small flat pods 1½ minutes or large flat pods 2 minutes. (If peas have started to develop, blanch 3 minutes. If peas are already developed, shell and follow directions for green peas.) Cool, drain, and fill containers, leaving a ½-inch headspace.

PEAS: ENGLISH OR GREEN

PREPARATION: Allow 2 to 2½ pounds per pint. Wash, shell, rinse, and drain.

HOW TO FREEZE: Blanch 1½ minutes; chill quickly. Fill containers, shaking down and leaving a ½-inch headspace.

PEPPERS, HOT

PREPARATION: Select firm jalapeño or other chile peppers; wash. Halve large peppers. Remove stems, seeds, and membranes. Place, cut sides down, on a foil-lined baking sheet. Bake in a 425°F oven for 20 to 25 minutes or until skins are bubbly and browned. Cover peppers or wrap in foil and let stand about 15 minutes or until cool. Pull the skins off gently and slowly using a paring knife.

HOW TO FREEZE: Package in freezer containers, with as little air as possible.

PEPPERS, SWEET

PREPARATION: Select firm green, bright red, or yellow peppers; wash. Remove stems, seeds, and membranes. Place, cut sides down, on a foil-lined baking sheet. Bake in a 425°F oven for 20 to 25 minutes or until skins are bubbly and browned. Cover peppers or wrap in foil and let stand about 15 minutes or until cool. Pull off the skins gently and slowly using a paring knife.

HOW TO FREEZE: Quarter large pepper pieces or cut in strips. Fill containers, leaving a ½-inch headspace. Or spread peppers in a single layer on a baking sheet; freeze until firm. Fill container, shaking to pack tightly and removing as much air as possible.

BEETS

PREPARATION: Allow 3 pounds (without tops) per quart. Trim off beet tops, leaving an inch of stem and roots to reduce bleeding of color. Scrub well. Cover with boiling water. Boil about 15 minutes or until skins slip off easily; cool. Peel; remove stem and root ends. Leave baby beets whole. Cut medium or large beets into ½-inch cubes or slices. Halve or quarter large slices.

HOW TO FREEZE: Cook unpeeled beets in boiling water until tender. (Allow 25 to 30 minutes for small beets; 45 to 50 minutes for medium beets.) Cool quickly in cold water. Peel; remove stem and root ends. Cut in slices or cubes. Fill containers, leaving a ½-inch headspace.

CARROTS

PREPARATION: Use 1- to 1¼-inch-diameter carrots (large carrots may be too fibrous). Allow 2 to 3 pounds per quart. Wash, trim, peel, and rinse again. Leave tiny ones whole; slice or dice the remainder.

HOW TO FREEZE: Blanch tiny whole carrots for 5 minutes and cut-up carrots for 2 minutes; cool quickly. Pack tightly into containers, leaving a ½-inch headspace.

CORN, CREAM-STYLE

PREPARATION: Allow 2 to 3 pounds per pint. Remove husks. Scrub with a vegetable brush to remove silks. Wash and drain.

HOW TO FREEZE: Cover ears with boiling water; return to boiling and boil 4 minutes. Cool quickly; drain. Use a sharp knife to cut off just the kernel tips, then scrape corn with a dull knife. Fill containers, leaving a ½-inch headspace.

CORN, WHOLE KERNEL

PREPARATION: Allow 4 to 5 pounds per quart. Remove husks. Scrub with a vegetable brush to remove silks. Wash and drain.

HOW TO FREEZE: Cover ears with boiling water; return to boiling and boil 4 minutes. Cool quickly; drain. Cut corn from cobs at two-thirds depth of kernels; do not scrape cobs. Fill containers, leaving a ½-inch headspace.

HERB FREEZING TIP

Some herbs keep their flavor when frozen. Simply clean the leaves, dry them, and put them in sealed plastic bags (remove all the air before sealing) or freeze them in an ice cube tray. These herbs freeze well: basil, borage, chives, dill, lemongrass, mint, oregano, sage, tarragon, and thyme.

Freezing Fruits

APPLES

PREPARATION: Allow 2½ pounds per quart. Select varieties that are crisp, not mealy, in texture. Peel and core; halve, quarter, or slice. Dip into ascorbic acid color-keeper solution; drain.

HOW TO FREEZE: Use syrup, sugar, or dry pack, leaving recommended headspace.

APRICOTS

PREPARATION: Allow 2 to 2½ pounds per quart. If desired, peel as for peaches, page 215. Prepare as for peaches.

HOW TO FREEZE: Peel as for peaches, page 215. Use a syrup, sugar, or water pack, leaving the recommended headspace.

BERRIES

PREPARATION: Allow ¾ to 1 pound per pint. Can or freeze blackberries, blueberries, currants, elderberries, gooseberries, huckleberries, loganberries, mulberries, and raspberries. Freeze (do not can) boysenberries and strawberries.

HOW TO FREEZE: Slice strawberries, if desired. Use a syrup, sugar, or dry pack, leaving the recommended headspace. Or place berries (strawberries, blueberries, raspberries) in a single layer on a baking pan and place them in the freezer. Once they're frozen, put the berries in freezer containers or plastic freezer bags and seal. Stored this way, berries will keep in the freezer up to 1 year.

PEARS

PREPARATION: Allow 2 pounds per quart. Peel, halve, and core. Treat with ascorbic acid color-keeper solution; drain.

HOW TO FREEZE: Not recommended.

PLUMS

PREPARATION: Allow 2 to 3 pounds per quart. Prick skin on two sides. Freestone varieties may be halved and pitted.

HOW TO FREEZE: Halve and pit. Treat with ascorbic acid color-keeper solution; drain well. Use a syrup pack. Remove excess air.

RHUBARB

PREPARATION: Allow 1½ pounds per quart. Discard leaves and woody ends. Cut into ½- to 1-inch pieces.

HOW TO FREEZE: Blanch for 1 minute; cool quickly and drain. Use a syrup or dry pack, leaving the recommended headspace. Or use a sugar pack of ½ cup sugar to 3 cups fruit. Remove excess air.

CHERRIES

PREPARATION: Allow 2 to 3 pounds per quart. If desired, treat with ascorbic acid color-keeper solution; drain. If unpitted, prick skin on opposite sides to prevent splitting.

HOW TO FREEZE: Use a syrup, sugar, or dry pack, removing excess air.

MELONS

PREPARATION: Allow about 4 pounds per quart for honeydew, cantaloupe, and watermelon.

HOW TO FREEZE: Use a syrup, sugar, or dry pack, removing excess air.

NECTARINES AND PEACHES

PREPARATION: Allow 2 to 3 pounds per quart. To peel peaches, immerse in boiling water for 20 to 30 seconds or until skins start to crack; remove and plunge into cold water. (Peeling nectarines is not necessary.) Halve and pit. If desired, slice. Treat with ascorbic acid color-keeper solution; drain.

HOW TO FREEZE: Use a syrup, sugar, or dry pack, leaving the recommended headspace.

Drying Basics

Easy and inexpensive, drying or dehydrating produce lets you savor the flavor of homegrown delights long after the harvest.

Using a dehydrator

Savor summer's overabundance of tomatoes, cucumbers, beans, and berries in soups and stews when you dehydrate the surplus. Dehydrating offers a host of benefits. It's considerably cheaper than buying dried fruit and vegetables in the store, where a 1-ounce container of dried tomato slices typically costs about $4 and a 1.5-ounce package of dried strawberries is around $6. Plus, dehydrated produce—which lasts for months—takes less storage space than canned or frozen food.

Best of all, dehydrated food keeps most of its flavor and nutritional value. According to the Food and Drug Administration, dehydrating retains 95 to 97 percent of the nutrients in fresh food. And it's faster and more convenient than sun-drying and more effective and energy-efficient than oven-drying.

Choosing a dehydrator

Dehydrators are simple machines that, at a touch of a button, remove the moisture from food with a small heater and fan that circulates air around a series of stackable trays.

Dehydrators are usually round or rectangular units that vary from $30 to $400—most in the $30 to $200 range. When purchasing one, consider how much food you regularly plan to dry. Some dehydrators hold just 4 pounds of food; others accommodate more than 30 pounds.

Check that trays are easy to load and stack in place and are simple to clean. Look for models with handy accessories, such as mesh inserts that prevent small pieces of food from falling through the trays.

Prepare the produce

The finished product is only as good as the original food, so use only the freshest produce available. Wash it thoroughly and cut away bruised or damaged portions. For quicker dehydration, peel the produce—unpeeled it can take up to twice as long to dry. Cut the produce into thin slices, generally about ⅛ to ¼ inch thick.

The next step depends on the type of produce you're drying. Some fruits, such as apples, pears, bananas, and peaches, need to be treated to prevent discoloration. After slicing, immediately soak them in a bowl of lemon, pineapple, or orange juice for 5 minutes. Or soak them in a mixture of 1 quart water and 1 teaspoon ascorbic acid, an antioxidant used in canning.

Fruits with a natural protective wax coating, such as grapes, blueberries, and cranberries, should be dipped into boiling water for a couple minutes before dehydrating to crack their coating and facilitate evaporation.

Most vegetables need to be steamed or blanched for a short time before drying to seal in their flavor and nutrients.

Dry your garden bounty

Place produce in the dehydrator, spreading slices evenly in a single layer on the tray, leaving a little space between pieces to promote air circulation. Set the temperatures—fruits are typically dried at 115°F and vegetables at 120°F, although you can adjust the temperature for slower or faster drying—then just push the button.

Expect vegetables to dry in 2 to 16 hours and fruits to dry in 4 to 48 hours. The more moisture in the fruit or vegetable, the longer it will take to dry. Avoid adding fresh pieces to a batch that's drying because it will lengthen the drying time.

To check whether produce has dried thoroughly—which is important to prevent mold—cut through the center of a slice with a knife. Allow dried produce to thoroughly cool.

Preparation Pointers

1 Core and slice the fruit into ¼-inch-thick slices for best results. After cutting the slices, immediately put them in a holding solution of lemon, pineapple, or orange juice and soak them for 5 minutes. To speed up the drying process, drain the slices on a paper towel to remove excess moisture before placing them in the dehydrator.

2 Place slices in the dehydrator in a single layer with space between pieces to provide proper ventilation for quicker drying.

Air Drying 101

DRYING HERBS
The traditional way to preserve herbs entails gathering small bunches of 10 to 15 stems and hanging them in a warm, well-ventilated place to dry. Wrap stems tightly with a rubber band or tie them with twine. Hang the bunches on a drying rack, on the rung of a hanger, or from a nail. Drying can take up to 3 weeks, depending on the plant and its moisture content. Strip crisp-dry leaves off stems before storing them.

DRYING PEPPERS
Drying hot peppers, such as jalapeños, is easy. Just cut off the stem of the pepper plant at ground level, then hang the entire plant—stems, leaves, and peppers—upside down in a cool, dark, dry location. The branching of the stems allows separation of the peppers so there is adequate airflow around them. Peppers retain their bright colors and hot flavor. Use care when handling hot peppers: Wear gloves and a dust mask.

STORE DRIED TREATS
Once produce is completely dried or dehydrated, package it immediately to prevent it from reabsorbing moisture. How dried produce is stored is as important as how it is dried. Glass jars with tight-fitting lids make the best storage containers. Also use freezer bags (regular plastic storage bags to not provide adequate protection).

Troubleshooting

Bugs, disease, birds, deer, and weather extremes—many things can eat or damage your garden. But if you plan and plant smart—as well as keep a sharp eye on your plantings—you can nip problems in the bud.

Battling Bugs

However much time and effort you put into your vegetable garden, there's always at least one insect that invades your homegrown harvests. Don't despair: Here's an easy guide to identifying—and conquering—those pesky vegetable bugs.

Insects are a gardening fact of life, but don't let them overrun your garden and make your hard work tending and growing vegetables be in vain. Here's a guide to avoiding and combating some of the most common insects you'll encounter.

Minimize the damage

Whether you start seeds or buy garden-center transplants, carefully read packages and labels. Choose resistant varieties and keep those plants vigorous and healthy so they're able to resist any pests that may come calling. Regular doses of plant food, adequate sunlight, and water during dry spells ensures healthy growth too.

What's the bug?

It's wise to regularly inspect plants for telltale holes or sick-looking stems. When you find evidence of an invasion, make sure the damage was caused by an insect rather than a disease or some other pest. Once you identify the pest, determine how much damage you and your plants can tolerate.

What's next?

Start by trying to reduce injury to your plants through physical protection or biological control; use a chemical control only when necessary. Control demands good timing, so learn a little bit about the insect's life cycle. Some methods are effective only at certain stages of an insect's life. If you must use chemicals, check the label first to ensure that both the plant you are treating and the insect you are trying to eliminate is listed.

Keep in mind that most insects have natural predators. Learn which ones are beneficial—including parasitic wasps, ladybugs, lacewings, predatory mites, fireflies, and predatory nematodes—and encourage them by planting their favorite host crops nearby. (Note: Many insecticides kill beneficial insects just as easily as harmful ones, so use them only as a last resort.)

Floating row covers keep young squash safe from cucumber beetles.

A cutworm collar protects a young broccoli plant from attack.

Look closely to see the insects bugging your plant, then treat for the specific type of pest.

FIELD GUIDE TO THE GARDEN'S

Most Unwanted

Your crops may be bugged by a variety of insects. The best advice is to find out the type of pest and treat only for that insect species.

EUROPEAN CORN BORER

Look for holes, wilting foliage, and broken stems as signs of this highly destructive pest.

WHAT IT EATS: Corn, tomatoes, potatoes, and peppers.

FIND IT: Look for brown-headed, pinkish caterpillars. The disgusting little pests burrow into vegetables, reducing them to a slimy mess. Corn leaves will be filled with tiny holes, tassels will be broken, and ear stalks will be bent.

CONTROL IT: Destroy egg masses; encourage beneficial insects such as ladybugs and wasps. Use Bt or a general-purpose insecticide until the borers vanish. Destroy plant material after the growing season.

SQUASH VINE BORER

Hubbard squash is a favorite; moths are metallic green, and larvae are white.

WHAT IT EATS: Squash, pumpkins, and gourds.

FIND IT: Although these worms burrow into plant stems and often don't reveal their damage until it's too late, you should still watch for small holes in the stems near ground level.

CONTROL IT: Carefully slit the stem of an infested vine and stab the worm before it causes too much damage, then cover the vine with soil to encourage rerooting. Head off damage by using floating row covers, attracting parasitic wasps, and rotating crops.

CABBAGE LOOPER/WORM

Lettuce is also a victim of this bug. Adults will lay eggs throughout the growing season; the moth is brownish and lays eggs on the upper surfaces of leaves. Look for round or irregular holes as telltale signs.

WHAT IT EATS: All members of the cabbage family.

FIND IT: Cabbageworms attach yellow eggs to the undersides of leaves and tunnel through heads; the white, mature butterflies fly around plants in the daytime. Cabbage looper moths lay pale green eggs in the evening.

CONTROL IT: Handpick the worms, use floating row covers, spray with an insecticide, or use insecticidal soap. Bt, a naturally occurring bacteria, can also be used when the insects are small.

SQUASH BUGS

Squash bugs are difficult to control; watch for brick red egg clusters on spring leaves of seedlings. Crushing them is your best bet, but it brings out an offensive odor, which gives them their nickname of stink bugs.

WHAT IT EATS: Squash.

FIND IT: These ugly brown bugs often appear en masse and suck juices right out of the plant leaves, causing them to wilt and turn black and brittle.

CONTROL IT: Attract parasitic wasps, use floating row covers, and handpick insects and their eggs (when crushed, they emit an offensive odor). Or lay a board on the ground and crush bugs that gather underneath. For severe infestations, try insecticidal soap or general-purpose insecticides; also look for resistant varieties.

COLORADO POTATO BEETLE

This insect resists treatment, so look for newly developed potato varieties that are resistant.

WHAT IT EATS: Potatoes, eggplants, peppers, and tomatoes.

FIND IT: Mature Colorado potato beetles are yellow-orange with black stripes; the insect lays its yellow-orange eggs on the undersides of leaves.

CONTROL IT: Handpick adults and egg masses, use floating row covers, or treat with a general-purpose insecticide. This pest not only eats holes in leaves but also can carry disease from one plant to another season.

CUCUMBER BEETLE

Two varieties of cucumber beetle—striped and spotted—carry mosaic and bacterial wilt. Destroy any infected plants because the bugs can overwinter in debris.

WHAT IT EATS: Cucumber, melons, pumpkins, and squash.

FIND IT: Look for holes in the leaves, stalks, and stems of vegetables. Watch for striped beetles, yellow-orange eggs, or white grubs.

CONTROL IT: The most effective solutions are to handpick and destroy the bugs, use floating row covers, and treat with a general-purpose insecticide. Cucumber beetles also spread bacterial wilt, a disease that causes the entire plant to go limp and die and for which there's no cure.

FLEA BEETLE

Although flea beetles jump like fleas, they bear no relation. The legless gray grubs and black mature beetles are tiny and feed primarily on roots and lower leaf surfaces.

WHAT IT EATS: Eggplants, potatoes, and peppers.

FIND IT: If you find tiny holes in the foliage that leave a bronzy leaf with little perforations, you have flea beetles.

CONTROL IT: Even with flea beetle infestations, a healthy vegetable plant will continue to produce. If you notice leaf damage, apply a general insecticide or insecticidal soap. Carefully check new leaves for damage and treat as needed. After growing season ends, clean up and discard any leftover plant matter.

APHIDS

Aphids come in a rainbow of colors—pale green, yellow, purple, or black. Infected leaves turn yellow; the common insect stunts plant growth.

WHAT IT EATS: Any and all.

FIND IT: Aphids, small and round in a variety of colors, usually appear in large numbers. They live by sucking juice of plant leaves and causing distorted, irregular growth.

CONTROL IT: Use floating row covers and attract beneficial insects. Or spray the insects off plants with a strong stream of water from a garden hose. For severe infestations, use an insecticidal soap or general-purpose insecticide.

SPIDER MITES

Look for dried-out, dropping leaves as well as webbing as clues that spider mites have invaded your vegetable patch.

WHAT IT EATS: Any and all.

FIND IT: Tiny spider mites suck juices out of plant leaves, giving the foliage a bronzy, stippled look. They make webs and hang out on the bottoms of leaves.

CONTROL IT: Spider mites are tough to deal with. Attract beneficial insects, or use an insecticidal soap or a general-purpose insecticide product.

CUTWORMS

If you dig down 2 inches around vegetables infected with cutworms, you'll find dull gray, brown, or black worms that are striped or spotted.

WHAT IT EATS: A range of plants, including beans, plants in the cabbage family, potatoes, and corn.

FIND IT: Infested seedlings look as if they are sawed off at ground level.

CONTROL IT: Use a 3-inch cardboard collar around young plant stems or apply a general-purpose insecticide.

An Ounce of Prevention

Healthy plants have the best chance of fighting off or withstanding insect damage. Follow these tips and you should see fewer problems.

APPLY ORGANIC MATTER each season to build healthy soil.

MULCH to eliminate insect-harboring weeds.

GROW VARIETIES adapted to your climate.

INSPECT PLANTS before buying them at local garden centers.

PLANT AT THE PROPER TIME to avoid stress from cold soil or air temperatures. Sometimes adjusting planting time can be enough to avoid damage from early- or late-feeding insects.

INSPECT PLANTS DAILY—examining both the tops and bottoms of leaves—to catch problems in their early stages, when they are easier to control.

ROTATE CROPS each year to avoid reinfection from insects that overwinter in the soil or on plant debris.

PLANT A "TRAP" CROP nearby to lure some insects away from your harvest crop. One especially well-fed and fertilized plant will attract pests quickly. Grow it away from your other plants; when it's infested, wrap it in plastic and throw it in the trash.

REMOVE AND DESTROY plants that are seriously damaged before insects can spread.

CLEAN UP ALL PLANT DEBRIS at the end of the growing season.

Deterring Other Pests

Protect your plants by learning how to identify the culprit(s), then tailor your response accordingly.

You see the damage to your garden, but you aren't sure of the cause. Here are some ways to determine what's eating your fruits and vegetables.

The tunnelers

Moles, voles, and gophers leave unsightly holes in lawns and garden beds. On the positive side, these animals help build the soil by turning it over and incorporating organic matter. Though moles, voles, and gophers all dig tunnels, they have little else in common. Moles (insectivores) rarely eat plants, preferring insects (including Japanese beetle grubs and cutworms). A 6-inch-long mole will ingest 70 to 80 percent of its body weight in insects every day. Voles (rodents) eat grasses, herbaceous plants, and seeds. Like moles, they consume almost their body weight in food daily. Gophers (rodents) consume roots, grasses, bulbs, and stems. The size of large rats, they use their cheek pouches to haul seeds and bark bits back to their subterranean dens.

Traps are available to catch the critters, but success may be as elusive as the animals themselves. (For particulars on traps appropriate for each critter, contact your county extension service.) A better bet to control moles is to cut off their food supply by reducing the grub population with a biological control such as milky spore disease (available in powdered form at garden supply stores). Deter voles by eliminating weeds, heavy mulch, and dense cover and by burying wire fencing 6 to 10 inches below ground. To thwart gophers, line planting holes with hardware cloth and protect garden beds with fencing buried 2 to 3 feet below ground.

Night raiders

At dusk many animals emerge from their dens and go looking for dinner. In nearly every state and southern Canada, rabbits seek tender new growth. If you suspect rabbits of damaging your plants, look for dark oval-shape droppings in small heaps. The rodents also leave scratch marks and small holes in freshly turned beds.

Foliar sprays are available, but 3-foot-high fences are the most reliable deterrents. Set the fence (chicken wire works well) 6 inches below ground to prevent burrowing. Wrap young trees in hardware cloth and plant onions (repulsive to rabbits) among favorite bunny fare. When all else fails, cultivate vegetables that rabbits don't like, such as squash, cucumbers, and corn.

Gardeners who plant corn could have other bandits—raccoons—to deal with. These opportunistic omnivores feast on homegrown vegetables, household garbage, rodents, and insects. Though their metabolism slows in winter, raccoons don't hibernate, making the quest for food a year-round affair. Homeowners should keep garbage cans inside overnight, because raccoons can manipulate lids and gate latches. Where raccoons are active, gardens should be caged, with a chicken-wire roof installed to protect corn plants. Other controls come with consequences. Trapped raccoons won't hesitate to bite or scratch, and they can carry rabies.

Usually raccoons are assumed to be responsible when corn crops are devoured. The fault may lie elsewhere, however. Squirrels, too, have a passion for corn and will climb stalks to get at tender ears. Unlike raccoons, who often break the stalks and feast on the spot, squirrels leave stalks intact and take their booty to a more secure location.

Oh, deer!

White-tailed deer number 25 million—and they love chowing down in small suburban yards and large farms across America. As the controversy rages over what should be done about the population explosion, gardeners respond in various ways. Nurseries stock an ever-growing array of repellents. Homemade deterrents such as locks of human hair and bars of soap hang from trees and posts on many properties, and radios blare in gardens 24 hours a day.

Protect the bark of young fruit trees with plastic. Deer and rabbits can nibble on bark and girdle a tree—which will kill the tree.

Bird netting keeps fruit-eating birds from ravaging your ripening crops.

Raccoons love corn, but these opportunistic omnivores will feast on other homegrown vegetables. Very adept at opening containers, they may also invade your compost bin in search of food.

FIELD GUIDE TO THE

Garden Foes

A number of neighborhood inhabitants may be eyeing your homegrown produce. Discover ways to deter them while protecting your harvest.

RABBITS

WHAT IT EATS: Rabbits will eat vegetable gardens and the tender shoots of young plants, including shrubs.

FIND IT: Look for nibbled-on vegetables or tree bark. Tell-tale black oval droppings let you know a rabbit has been noshing on your greens.

CONTROL IT: A fence is the most effective way to exclude rabbits from your yard. Welded wire mesh at the base of a fence will deter even small young rabbits. For small vegetable and herb beds, make a lightweight frame and cover it with plastic mesh netting.

DEER

WHAT IT EATS: Gardeners spend a lot of time and effort trying to outwit these hungry grazers. Deer can denude a garden of just about everything (usually your favorite plants); keeping them out of your garden is important. Deer like fruit trees and eat windfall fruit as well as stand on their hind legs to graze on leaves.

FIND IT: Look for nibbled produce, hoof prints in moist garden soil, and round black droppings.

CONTROL IT: Many products deter deer. Most are scent-based sprays or liquids that make an area or plant undesirable. Others attempt to startle deer with sprays of water. The best defense is a barrier—an 8-foot fence around the perimeter of your garden.
.

SQUIRRELS

WHAT IT EATS: Squirrels are known to invade vegetable gardens and eat ripening tomatoes and cucumbers. They love sunflower seeds, so if you are growing these big-headed blooms for the seeds, keep an alert eye out.

FIND IT: Squirrels generally cart off their food instead of eating it onsite. Squirrels prefer to launch their raids at sunset and daybreak. These pesky rodents also dig up flower bulbs after fall planting.

CONTROL IT: To protect ripening crops, create a fence around your enclosure and place netting over the top (squirrels are excellent climbers, so cover all angles of entry). Use netting or mesh fine enough (1 inch square or smaller) to keep small animals out.

BIRDS

WHAT IT EATS: Fruit-eating birds, such as robins, devour ripening fruit such as cherries, blueberries, and strawberries.

FIND IT: Disappearing fruit may be your first clue.

CONTROL IT: Lightweight netting can be draped over trees, bushes, or individual plants without causing plant damage. If you have an orchard, set up a frame to create a roof of netting that will protect a large area.

Build a Pest-Proof Fence

USE FENCES TO DETER RABBITS AND DEER. IF THE GARDEN IS NOT IN A RAISED BED, MAKE SURE THE BOTTOM OF THE FENCE EXTENDS ABOUT 6 INCHES UNDER THE SOIL TO STOP RABBITS FROM DIGGING BENEATH IT. A FENCE NEEDS TO STAND AT LEAST 8 FEET ABOVE THE GROUND TO PREVENT DEER FROM JUMPING OVER IT.

1 Drive in posts at each corner of the raised bed.

2 Add eye hooks to the tops of the posts. String wire for top support.

3 Add eyehooks to raised bed base.

4 Attach netting to posts, top wire support, and raised bed base.

The USDA Plant Hardiness
Zone Map

Each plant has an ability to withstand cold temperatures, called a hardiness rating. This range of temperatures is expressed as a zone—and a zone map shows where you can grow this plant.

Planting for your zone

There are 11 zones from Canada to Mexico, and each zone represents the lowest expected winter temperature in that area. Each zone is based on a 10-degree difference in minimum temperatures. Once you know your hardiness zone, you can choose plants for your garden that will flourish. Look for the hardiness zone on the plant tags of the perennials, trees, and shrubs you buy.

Microclimates in your yard

Not all areas in your yard are the same. Depending on your geography, trees, and structures, some spots may receive different sunlight and wind and consequently experience temperature differences. Take a look around your yard and you may notice that the same plant comes up sooner in one place than another. This is the microclimate concept in action. A microclimate is an area in your yard that is slightly different (cooler or hotter) than the other areas of your yard.

Create a microclimate

Once you're aware of your yard's microclimates, you can use them to your advantage. For example, you may be able to grow plants in a sheltered, south-facing garden bed that you can't grow elsewhere in your yard. You can create a microclimate by planting evergreens on the north side of a property to block prevailing winds. Or plant deciduous trees on the south side to provide shade in summer.

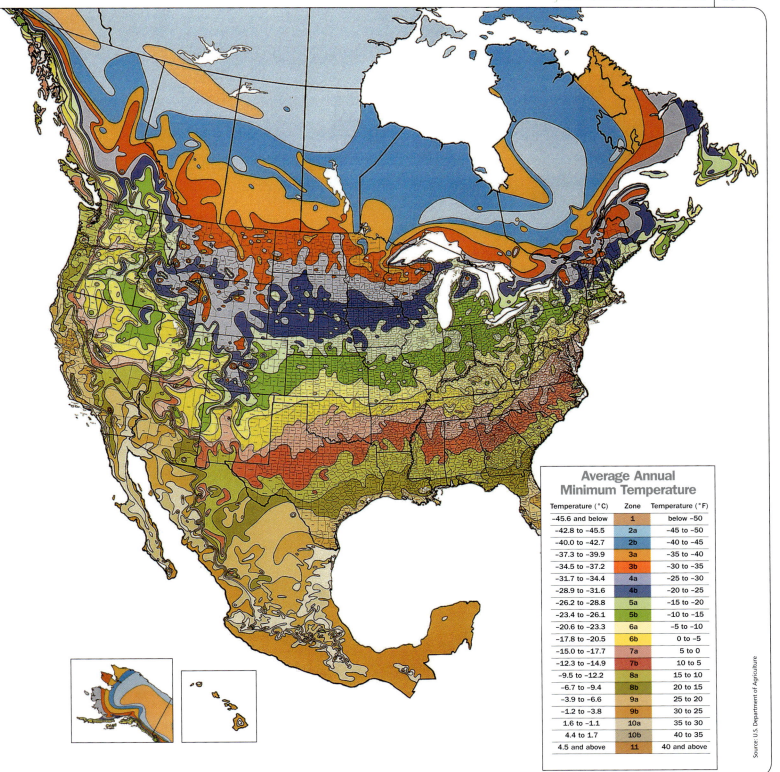

Average Annual Minimum Temperature

Temperature (°C)	Zone	Temperature (°F)
–45.6 and below	1	below –50
–42.8 to –45.5	2a	–45 to –50
–40.0 to –42.7	2b	–40 to –45
–37.3 to –39.9	3a	–35 to –40
–34.5 to –37.2	3b	–30 to –35
–31.7 to –34.4	4a	–25 to –30
–28.9 to –31.6	4b	–20 to –25
–26.2 to –28.8	5a	–15 to –20
–23.4 to –26.1	5b	–10 to –15
–20.6 to –23.3	6a	–5 to –10
–17.8 to –20.5	6b	0 to –5
–15.0 to –17.7	7a	5 to 0
–12.3 to –14.9	7b	10 to 5
–9.5 to –12.2	8a	15 to 10
–6.7 to –9.4	8b	20 to 15
–3.9 to –6.6	9a	25 to 20
–1.2 to –3.8	9b	30 to 25
1.6 to –1.1	10a	35 to 30
4.4 to 1.7	10b	40 to 35
4.5 and above	11	40 and above

Source: U.S. Department of Agriculture

Buying Guide and
Resources

For information about sourcing seeds, plants, and gardening products, contact these resources.

PLANT INFORMATION WEBSITES

Ball Seed
ballhort.com

Better Homes and Gardens
bhg.com

American Horticulture Society
ahs.org 703/768-5700

American Rose Society
ars.org

Perennial Plant Association
perennialplant.org 614/771-8431

International Flower Bulb Centre
bulb.com

MAIL-ORDER PLANTS

Busse Gardens
bussegardens.com 800/544-3192

Forestfarm
forestfarm.com 541/846-7269

Gilbert H. Wild & Son, L.L.C
gilberthwild.com 888/449-4537

Greer Gardens
greergardens.com 800/548-0111

High Country Gardens
highcountrygardens.com 800/925-9387

Jackson & Perkins
jacksonandperkins.com 800/292-4769

Musser Forests
musserforests.com 800/643-8319

Niche Gardens
nichegardens.com 919/967-0078

Plant Delights Nursery
plantdelights.com 919/772-4794

Tranquil Lake Nursery
tranquil-lake.com 508/252-4002

Under A Foot Plant Company (Stepables)
stepables.com 503/581-8915

Van Bourgondien
dutchbulbs.com 800/622-9997

White Flower Farm
whiteflowerfarm.com 800/503-9624

MAIL-ORDER SEEDS

W. Atlee Burpee & Company
burpee.com 800/333-5808

Ferry-Morse Seed Company
ferry-morse.com 800/626-3392

Gurney's Seed and Nursery
gurneys.com 513/354-1492

Johnny's Selected Seeds
johnnyseeds.com 877/564-6697

Nichols Garden Nursery
gardennursery.com 800/422-3985

Park Seed Company
parkseed.com 800/213-0076

Pinetree Garden Seeds
superseeds.com 207/926-3400

Renee's Garden
reneesgarden.com 888/880-7228

Richters
richters.com 905/640-6677

Seeds of Change
seedsofchange.com 888/762-7333

Seed Savers Exchange
seedsavers.org 563/382-5990

Select Seeds
selectseeds.com 800/684-0395

Stokes Seeds
stokeseeds.com 800/396-9238

Thompson & Morgan
thompson-morgan.com 800/274-7333

The Cook's Garden
cooksgarden.com 800/457-9703

The Gourmet Gardener
gourmetgardener.com 386/362-9089

YARD AND GARDEN SUPPLIES

Charley's Greenhouse & Garden
charleysgreenhouse.com
800/322-4707

Duncraft
duncraft.com 888/879-5095

Gardener's Supply Company
www.gardeners.com 888/833-1412

Kinsman Company
kinsmangarden.com 800/733-4146

Index